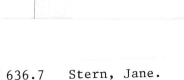

ALSO BY JANE AND MICHAEL STERN

Dog Eat Dog

Amazing America

American Gourmet

Auto Ads

Douglas Sirk (*by Michael Stern*)

Elvis World

The Encyclopedia of Bad Taste

Friendly Relations

Goodfood

Happy Trails: Our Life Story (*with Roy Rogers and Dale Evans*)

Horror Holiday

Jane and & Michael Stern's Encycopedia of Pop Culture

Real American Food

Roadfood

Roadfood and Goodfood

Sixties People

Square Meals

A Taste of America

Trucker: A Portrait of the Last American Cowboy (*by Jane Stern*)

Way Out West

Where to Eat in Connecticut

Being the authentic story of two very different young dogs, one who is virtuous and goes on to a life of service, the other born to be naughty and wreak havoc in her loving owner's home . . . including much practical advice for anyone considering life with a puppy.

Two Puppies

Jane and Michael Stern

SCRIBNER

SCRIBNER
1230 Avenue of the Americas
New York, NY 10020

DESIGNED BY ERICH HOBBING
Set in Adobe Garamond

Manufactured in the United States of America

10 9 8 7 6 5 4 3 2 1

Library of Congress Cataloging-in-Publication Data

Stern, Jane
Two puppies/Jane and Michael Stern
p.   cm
Includes bibliographical references.
1. Puppies—Anecdotes. 2. Dog owners—Anecdotes. 3. Human–animal relationships—
Anecdotes. 4. Stern, Jane. 5. Stern, Michael. 6. Puppies. I. Stern, Michael, date. II. Title.

SF426.2.S74 1998   98–34649
636.7—dc21   CIP

ISBN 0-684-83752-8

For Bunny Kyle,
to whom we dedicate
this book in lieu of combat pay

ACKNOWLEDGMENTS

Much as we enjoy the company of dogs, it has been a special pleasure spending time with so many dog-loving humans.

The staff at Guiding Eyes for the Blind in Yorktown Heights, New York, were kind enough to let us sit in on nearly every phase of their extraordinary work breeding and training guide dogs, then pairing them with blind people. Thanks to Bill Badger for opening the door, Steve Kuusisto for sharing his story with such eloquence, Kathy and Ted Zubrycki for their wisdom regarding all creatures great and small, Sue McCahill and Jessica Sanchez for allowing us to be present for their remarkable training sessions, and Russ Post for helping us understand the in-for-training tests. We are so grateful to Dan and Susan Fisher-Owens for telling us about their life with young Parnell and sharing his baby pictures. Jane Russenberger gave us a grand tour of the Breeding Center and was kind enough to invite us to a conference with the greatest stud of all, Sailor. Finally, we owe a special debt of gratitude to Guiding Eyes' class of January, 1997, for allowing us to share a small part of their extraordinary journey from darkness to independence. We love you, Esther Acha, Cindy Blair, Rosario Cura, Alison Dolan, Murry Dimon, Craig Hedgecock, Thomas Massa, Spencer McMillan, Bob Serrano, Linette Stevens, Henry Tucker, and Joyce Whitney!

Special thanks to our friend Mimi Einstein, who is always ready to help in any dog-related crisis. We also want to thank Bunny Kyle and Jean Wagner for toughing it out when the going got tough with our Darling Clementine.

It is often said that editors no longer have time to really edit a manuscript. Not so of Susan Moldow, who cared about this book every bit as much as we did, and whose advice and editorial wisdom has kept our own creative flame burning. Thanks also to Kim Kanner, for always being there to make things happen, publishing-wise. Binky Urban, our agent and a vexatious-puppy veteran herself, lent support as well as sympathy throughout.

Finally, a big, loving hug to Allstar's Darling Clementine who, despite the cataclysmic wild youth of which we write in the following pages, has grown into a devoted and soulful creature we are proud to call our girl.

Information Sidebars

FOREWORD

Puppies are a promise so magical that in no small part because of them man decided to leave the cave between fourteen and fifteen thousand years ago, invent agriculture, and launch our species into our spectacular modern era. Hyperbole? I don't think so.

Four animals were domesticated at nearly the same time, that was during the Paleolithic, the Old Stone Age, and they set mankind loose from his cavebound past. Those mighty four (we are not really certain of the sequence) were the goat, the sheep, the wolf/dog and—can you guess?—the reindeer. Then came agriculture, probably invented by women.

Consider this: If you discount your own biological cycling, nutrition, ingestion and discarding, procreation, all those kinds of things, name one thing that you and I do today that our ancestral cave folks did. The only thing you are likely to come up with that is not integral to your own bodily survival is reaching out and patting your canine companion. That is the oldest and most normal thing we do.

How did wolves-cum-dogs help us up and out of the cave? They made the keeping of the other critical domesticates practical. We could keep sheep, goats, and reindeer, sources of meat, hides, and later, milk, in large numbers. And keeping them in herds and flocks because we had dogs to help us meant we could feed ever larger concentrations of people, therefore cities could grow and prosper.

But what of that promise I mentioned at the beginning? Simple enough: Puppies promise us that they will be neotonous. That less-than-poetic word is a scientific term (very few scientific terms are poetic, poetic terms represent an emotional use of language, and to science emotions are anathema) that means the retention of juvenile characteristics into adult years. Puppies promise us they will never grow up. They will always be our furry kids and retain their endearing puppyhood traits.

Endearing traits, are they? What is so endearing that we can willingly overlook a pile of poop beside our bed in the morning, the puddle on the oriental rug, and the bedroom slipper in shreds? Well, first of all, a puppy's eyes look straight ahead, just as ours do. Puppies have milk breath and that is practically an aphrodisiac for animal lovers! Puppies giggle—or approximately so—when we tickle them, they curl up against us when they sleep, they are soft and warm and love to have their bellies rubbed. They make silly little feisty sounds when we play roughhouse games with them and, above all, they need us. They will play our games, run in our pack, and always be close to us. Our children will grow up; our puppies never will, not really.

Is it any wonder, then, that man began keeping some of the beguiling little wolf cubs he captured alive and by his side? Is it any wonder he kept the most endearing of them alive yet longer? Since he probably (make that *certainly*) had totems he allowed breeding between the most endearing of all. And which were those? The ones that didn't bite the kids or try to eat Aunt Millie—the easy-keepers. We have always sought out the easy-keepers. And the totem idea gave us preferred physical characteristics, including color and perhaps size. When man knew nothing about DNA and genes and chromosomes he was breeding selectively without the foggiest idea of what he was doing.

And so today we have hundreds of breeds worldwide, all largely wolf descendants (a small subspecies from Asia and Asia Minor, *Canis lupes pallipes*), possibly as many as 850 breeds, and they all start out as puppies (same thing as cubs in their earlier wolf phase) and they all make the same promises, be they chihuahua or St. Bernard, one weighing at least a hundred times as much as the other: *We will never grow up and you will never not be needed.*

Jane and Michael Stern explore this incredible bonding with their own special way of looking at matters canine. You just can't beat this mix—insight, humor, and dogs, especially puppy dogs. Go forward, have fun—that's what both dogs and the Sterns are for.

—ROGER A. CARAS

Two
Puppies

Buy a pup and your money will buy
Love unflinching that cannot lie
—RUDYARD KIPLING

INTRODUCTION

God created wolves, but dogs were made by human beings. *Canis familiaris*—the domesticated pet so many of us love and depend on—is a glorious and sometimes disturbing result of humankind's will to meddle with nature.

The evolution of man's best friend out of *Canis lupis* began during the Stone Age when our ancestors figured out that wolves might be handy companions. They could chase and corner game better than a biped; and they performed the useful service of after-dinner cleanup: eating leftovers and gnawing bones gleaming white. At the same time, wolves realized that keeping company with *homo sapiens* meant shelter, warmth, and a nice scratch behind the ears from time to time.

In the twenty-five millennia since that happy prehistoric union, dogs have been domesticated and designed with exquisite precision to live with us, work alongside us, go to war for us, amuse us, and comfort us.

Human history is filled with dogs, going back to the Egyptian god Anubis, son of Osiris, who had a jackal's head and was in charge of weighing dead pharaohs' hearts. A few millennia later, William of Normandy's conquest of England was abetted by packs of fighting mastiffs at his warhorses' sides. Medieval European culture as well as ancient Asian civilizations are rich with images of dogs carved on tombs, gladiators' shields, and heraldic crests. Like the Norse superheroes who expected to enter Valhalla accompanied by their warrior dogs, many of history's dog devotees endowed the canine race with exalted duties beyond this world: guardian of heaven's gate or the river Styx, or guides who shepherd souls to heaven.

Not all societies have considered dogs valued companions. In some cases they were food, and a plump puppy was as delicate a morsel as a cocktail cheese puff. Calvin Schwabe's book *Unmention-*

able Cuisine notes that Roman epicures considered suckling puppy a dish fit for the gods and that Hippocrates advocated dog meat as a health tonic. More recently, one of the lesser reasons Mao was so venerated by his followers during the Long March was his excellent recipe for stir-fried puppy with ginger and garlic. Before World War II, a favorite Hawaiian delicacy was stone-cooked puppy, for which a bunch of small carcasses are wrapped in leaves and nestled in hot stones like a Yankee clambake.

We late-twentieth-century dog fanciers have so incorporated canines into our family lives that cooking and eating one seems almost as taboo as cannibalism. To be a dog fancier does not mean you lick your lips at the sight of a well-marbled young Springer Spaniel, but rather that you appreciate the spaniel's role as a friend or helpmate.

Every breed of dog, old or new, was created to perform a task—to hunt, to guard, to track, or simply to amuse. And although the majority of dogs today are bought as house pets and never called upon to fulfill their genetic destiny, those very specific traits and talents are what make aficionados appreciate their chosen breed. Few people who acquire a Newfoundland puppy will expect it to pull large ships along a canal, as Newfies once did, but the big dog's strength and persistence still do serve us humans in search-and-rescue work. Nor does the average purchaser of a Silky Terrier expect their handsome little pup to spend its life catching rats (as the breed was originally intended to do), but its quickness and vigilance are still very much what make it so adored.

This book is about two purebred puppies of breeds that were designed for very specific tasks and are therefore as "man-made" as any dog can be: a Labrador Retriever originally created as a hunting companion, and a Bullmastiff, first bred to guard large estates from the predations of poachers. Although many labs still go hunting and many Bullmastiffs are expected to guard their masters' homes, both breeds are generally bought by people who simply want nice pets. In the case of our two subjects, however, each was destined for a higher purpose than mere friendship.

Parnell the Labrador Retriever is a service animal bred to guide the blind. Clementine the Bullmastiff was created in the expectation

20

she would win glory in the show ring. As you shall read, Parnell has nobly fulfilled his purpose; Clementine, sorry to say, did not develop the way her human breeders had hoped; in fact, she is a disaster.

Parnell is the progeny of generations of scientifically winnowed DNA plus the efforts of a team of expert human wards and trainers who molded his personality once he was born (at the cost of approximately twenty-five thousand dollars). By the time Parnell matured from puppyhood to doghood he had become a highly sensitive, finely tuned creature able to offer a blind woman not only the gifts of sight and of freedom but also a very special kind of companionship seldom achieved in any other human-animal relationship.

Clementine the Bullmastiff was bred in anticipation that she would be a superior example of her breed. Her distant forebears, the Bulldog and mastiff, were originally cross-bred in the nineteenth century to create a dog that would be a companion for gamekeepers on large estates in England. A massive, dark-coated beast, the Bullmastiff was designed to roam moor and dale, ever watchful but not ferocious. In the late twentieth century, the working Bullmastiff has been replaced by electronic security systems; but like so many breeds whose skills have become obsolete, it is a dog still treasured as a pet. Modern fanciers of the breed enjoy all the qualities that originally made the Bullmastiff such a fine "gamekeeper's night dog," especially its staunch but easygoing temper.

Clementine's birth was meticulously planned, the result of mating a stud and a dam of proven high merit in the expectation they would produce a litter of Bullmastiffs that exemplified the breed standard in both looks and personality. If she had turned out that way, she would likely have become a show dog, and would herself, in turn, have been bred to produce even more refined examples of the breed. But unlike the story of Parnell, the results of this breeding were far from what was expected. Despite her esteemed progenitors, Clementine looked weird and acted even weirder. She is proof that when man attempts to play genetic God, odd things can happen.

We can speak frankly about Clementine because she is our dog. She came into our home when she was six weeks old, at almost the same age the virtuous Parnell was selected to become a guide dog. From the beginning, Clementine was no paragon of virtue. In her story you will see two fairly peaceful human beings (us) brought to the brink of insanity and Bullmastifficide.

We believe it is a good thing to share our experiences raising her because they taught us valuable lessons about the complex dance of domesticated canine and human being. (Also, like all survivors of traumatic events, we *need* to share our experiences lest they drive us mad.) One thing we learned for certain is that no puppy is a blank slate on which its breeders or masters create the precise creature they want. Each comes complete with its own personality, talents, weaknesses, and quirks. Like children, puppies develop personalities out of an enigmatic blend of nature-and-nurture, with a good measure of potluck thrown into the mix.

In addition to the stories of Parnell and Clementine, we have included in this book information about selecting and living with a puppy: where to find one, how the experts determine future temperament (and how you can use these methods yourself), how to raise a puppy well, a survey of potential canine medical costs (which shocked the heck out of us when we added up the numbers), and thoughts from a number of well-known animal experts on how to raise and train a dog.

Two Puppies is a book we lived as we wrote. Like new parents everywhere, we found that much of what happened to us was startlingly different than the how-to manuals said it would be. We searched in vain for a book that was honest enough to tell us that sometimes dogs, like kids, don't grow up exactly as you want them to, despite your best intentions. We couldn't find such a book, so we wrote this one.

We had no idea where *Two Puppies* would wind up when we started it—didn't know if the ending would be happy or sad. We can tell you this: writers of fiction do not have the market cornered on strange twists of fate; real life is at least as much of a whirlwind. So as Bette Davis said in *All About Eve,* "Fasten your seatbelts. It's going to be a bumpy night."

CLEMENTINE:

ROSEMARY'S PUPPY

The first time we saw our new puppy Clementine she was two weeks old and half the size of her litter mates.

Runt is an ugly word, but political correctness has yet to make inroads in the dog world. The Bullmastiff puppy that lay before us on a tasteful slice of Berber carpet in the bedroom of a dog breeder's home in eastern Connecticut could not honestly be described as petite, downsized, compact, bantam, or weight-challenged. While her seven strapping siblings were each already fat double handfuls of robust puppy blubber, this Lilliputian oddball was hardly the size of a hamster. Not every litter of newborn puppies has a runt, but this one most certainly did, and she was it.

Her deficient size was not the only thing rodentlike about her. To the dismay of the dog breeder who planned this litter, the dark brindle girl also featured a big white stripe down the middle of her face: a calamity in a breed for which the standard specifies NO WHITE MARKINGS allowed anywhere other than on the chest.

"She looks like a little skunk," we exclaimed when we saw her, and from the slightly pained look on the breeder's face we knew our comment was not original. Clementine's small size and the white stripe on her face were anomalies to this breed; but paradoxically, the likelihood that these undesirable traits might get passed into the gene pool like a rampant virus were what brought us to look at this puppy in the first place.

We have great affection for Bullmastiffs, having owned four of them before we met Clementine. Each of our dogs was selected to serve no higher purpose than to be a beloved home companion, to sit quietly on the couch, look fondly at us, snuggle at our feet on a cold night, and wait patiently by the side of the bed for us to rise in the morning. This job description was a cushy one: no hunting, no guarding, no guiding, no finding lost children, no retrieving ducks, nothing required except being calm, gentle, and adorable.

And so we were easy-to-satisfy puppy shoppers. Our prerequisites were simple. The puppy of our dreams should look enough like a Bullmastiff to please us aesthetically, but be imperfect enough—compared to the official breed standard—that we would feel no pressure from the breeder to show or breed it. We were always clear on this subject—we didn't want a show-ring champion—and each of the dogs we had owned had been spayed or neutered routinely when it reached the proper age, usually before it was six months old. Our only other concern was that the dog we buy be reasonably sound. Although we know that good health is generally more common among mixed breeds that have the strength of biodiversity behind them, we were still confident that we could find a robust purebred with none of the common faults that muddy the purebred gene pool, which, in the case of Bullmastiffs means cancer, skeletal ills, and chronic skin problems.

Over the years we had come to adore the superficial imperfections of our nonshow dogs. Unlike the paragons of breed beauty that win blue ribbons, our pets were unique. Each was big and wrinkly and earnest enough to qualify as a Bullmastiff; but Minerva had a head as pointy as a dunce cap; Beulah's huge torso was perched on spindly legs; Gus's ears hung alongside his head like shriveled red peppers; and Edwina's muzzle was as long as a crocodile's. A Frenchman would call them "jolies-Laides": beautiful-ugly.

We were thrilled when our friend and Bullmastiff breeder Mimi Einstein told us about a recent litter sired by her magnificent stud Sam that featured a particularly goofy-looking puppy that might fit in nicely to our family of canine irregulars. Because of the white mark on her face, she would never be bred; nevertheless, she did come from a distinguished family of fine show dogs with personalities as beautiful as their buff exteriors.

Mimi's buoyant introduction brought us with high hopes to the home of the breeder in eastern Connecticut to look at the puppy when it was two weeks old. At first glance, the runt seemed perfect for us. She was kind of cute in a weird hamsterish way, and because of her deficient size and striped face, there would be no pressure to make her into anything but a happy couch potato. She was also less expensive then the fine fat fellows that shared her whelping box. She was a canine factory second.

Although she seemed to fill the bill perfectly when we saw her that first time, we now both can recall hearing a little voice whispering from our unconscious minds, a voice we then chose to ignore because we were blinded by desire for a new puppy. Even now it would be hard to tell exactly what it was about this little animal that made us uncomfortable, but in retrospect we believe that there was something almost eerie lurking behind her atypical features. In the months to come we would learn all too well just how strange a creature she really was. Still not yet ten pounds, she would soon plunge us headlong into the kind of confusion and frustration that, as smug veteran dog owners, we were certain we had left far behind in our past. When we went shopping for a cute little dog to love, we believed we knew just what we were doing.

So how is it that we found ourselves living with the devil disguised as a tiny round-eyed weanling, an animal that turned our lives into a living hell and finally taught us more about the strange and demanding affinity between dog and owner than we ever hoped to know?

PARNELL:

BLACK ANGEL

In July 1995, a seven-week-old black Labrador Retriever named Parnell was evaluated by a team of people who are experts in canine character.

They gathered around the roly-poly being and noted his lively expression and inquisitive nature, as well as a readiness to forgive someone who held him down and restrained him several seconds against his will.

They purposely tried to scare the little puppy by snapping open an umbrella in front of his face. Parnell, who was scampering freely on a linoleum floor, skidded to a stop and cocked his head. He was curious. The testers rested the open umbrella in his path and tried to coax him onto its web. At first, he wanted no part of it, but soon curiosity overwhelmed apprehension. Parnell climbed on, and when the umbrella rocked underneath his weight, he froze. But his tail stayed high and his ears stayed perked and almost instantly he returned to his examination of the strange, wobbly object.

The sudden rattle of a can full of coins made the tiny creature momentarily drop his tail out of fear, but again, his curiosity drew him toward the frightening noise to sniff it out. Soon, the tail was up and wagging, fear forgotten.

Parnell was very much enjoying his test, even the scary parts. He especially was thrilled to follow after anyone who strolled briskly around the room; he delighted in chasing after a towel that one of the testers dragged along the floor; and he was totally relaxed, even quite cheerful, when someone immobilized him by picking him up—he was no more than a handful—and holding him away from their chest, straight-armed in the air, thus preventing him from continuing his explorations.

After a half hour of such scrutiny, the people testing Parnell concluded that he was bright, willing, and resilient—all good qualities. On the other hand, they noted a strong affection for people, a devotion so intense that it could develop into servility. By nature, most puppies are submissive to a degree—toward their mother or toward the humans who care for them—and Parnell's apparent willingness to please is a charming quality many people treasure in an adult pet dog. But for what this young puppy was fated to do, a too dependent nature would have been an insurmountable handicap. A guide dog for the blind needs to lead, not follow.

Parnell was born to a life of service. Generations of his forebears were guide dogs and his father and his mother produced dozens of puppies that grew up to lead blind people through the world.

All of us are familiar with the concept of a guide dog, but guide dogs are surprisingly rare. Less than two percent of all Americans who are legally blind have one. There are many reasons their number is so small. Some people are too infirm to take advantage of the mobility a dog provides; some have too much vision to depend on a guide dog—they second-guess their dog's decisions, making a working relationship impossible; and many simply don't want the responsibilities that dog owning entails. For those who do learn to go through life with a guide dog, the difference that it makes can be a thing of wonder, and the relationship between such a dog and its master becomes one of extraordinary mutual reliance, closer and stronger than any other kind of human-animal bond.

Parnell was destined for such a life even before he was conceived. He was one of a litter of thirteen Labs out of a seasoned brood bitch named Jersey, by a veteran sire named Naples, both of which were dismissed from reproductive duties shortly after the thirteen-pup litter of May 23, 1995, which produced Parnell. Naples was retired because his sperm had begun to lose motility, Jersey because she put so much into her milk when whelping the puppies that she grew alarmingly thin.

The coupling of Naples and Jersey took place at the Guiding Eyes for the Blind Breeding Center in Patterson, New York, where the puppies were born and where Jersey took care of them for their first two months of life. During that two months, the brood bitch and puppies are observed constantly by a human staff who follow after them with notepads recording their growth and behavior. The breeding center, which is also where seven-week-old Parnell underwent his evaluation, used to be a private home set back on a hill over Route 164. Still a pleasant house surrounded by Putnam County's green foliage and unspoiled countryside, it has since been expanded and remodeled to house office space, kennels, whelping rooms, veterinary equipment, and a sophisticated reproduction laboratory. The front room of the building, where puppies are tested at the age of seven weeks, is festooned with distinguished eight-by-ten color photographic portraits of mature, handsome Labs, Golden Retrievers, and German Shepherds, each identified by its pedigreed name, which always begins with the words *Guiding Eyes FT Blind,* then the call name of the dog: Guiding Eyes FT Blind Holland, Guiding Eyes FT Blind Oakley, etc. In the adjacent kitchen, a "Wall of Fame" is reserved for photographs of dams and studs who have produced dozens of successful puppies, many of which have themselves become breeding stock. The picture of one recently retired sire of whom the staff speaks with reverence and heartfelt affection, is captioned "Father of 271 puppies"; Guiding Eyes FT Blind Mona is listed as the "Mother of 36." It is a moving experience to stand amidst the faces of so many dogs who have done so much to help people. Like canine gods, they radiate the power of their goodness.

None of these dogs, including Parnell's parents, Jersey and Naples, live full-time at the breeding center. They all reside with nearby "Harbor Families" who chaperone Guiding Eyes breeding stock—a total of one hundred bitches and thirty-eight studs altogether. The families pay the food bills and give each dog a normal home life; but for veterinary care or when it comes time for them to mate or to give birth, they are brought back to the center in Patterson. "For the bitches, we are like a hospital to which a pregnant woman goes just before her due date," says Jane Russenberger, director of the program. Jane is a sporty-looking woman in her thirties who is a veritable fount of genetic knowledge, able to reel off chromosomal data on her dogs like a hellfire preacher shouting scripture. What she doesn't have at the tip of her tongue is readily available in the infinitesimally detailed data books on Guiding Eyes shelves where Jane and her staff have recorded every possible statistic about a dog's or bitch's health, temperament, and suitability for breeding. "The dads might come in just for a quickie one afternoon or stay three or four days if we are doing a lot of breeding," Jane explains. Dads also drop by on occasion to make deposits in the sperm bank.

The purpose of the Guiding Eyes Breeding Center is to produce dogs that are physically sound and have a personality suited for guide work. Copious data are kept on the physical and mental progress of every puppy born; the information is related to the parents and to ancestors of that puppy to determine if those bloodlines and that particular cross of lines are fruitful. "Confidence is the hardest thing to breed for," Ms. Russenberger says. "Mostly because it is so complicated. We have found that insecurity with noises is inherited separately from insecurity with other dogs. And although much can be done to steer a puppy during its upbringing, all the training in the world cannot fix a dog that is genetically insecure."

Temperament is vital in a service dog; so is good health. Genetic data are used to track such critical qualities as skeletal integrity, vision, heart function, and general physical conformation. Performance of the thyroid, which regulates so much metabolic activity, is particularly important to track on a generation-to-generation chart, for a thyroid that is overactive or underactive (and therefore the potential cause for scores of metabolic problems from dermatitis to obesity) may not become apparent in an individual dog until well into its maturity.

Healthy as they are, not all guide dogs fit the official physical standard of their breed as published by the American Kennel Club and as rewarded in show rings with blue ribbons. Beauty is not the issue in these creatures who, after all, will spend their lives with people who cannot see them; ability is all that matters. So the fact that Parnell was missing four premolars or that his eyes have a light cinnamon hue or his head is fairly broad—"flaws" that might knock him out of competition in the show ring—had no bearing on his potential as a guide dog. Far more important were the facts that X rays revealed his hips to be sound and free from dysplasia, his eyes, heart, and skin were all in tip-top shape. It was noted that his sex organs were fine, too: an important factor if, in his full maturity, it was determined that Parnell was so excellent in temperament and conformation that he should serve as a stud instead of a working guide dog.

At seven weeks old, Parnell showed so much promise in his puppy test. He was as close to a perfect dog as eugenic science can create. His destiny, to help the human race, was still far ahead of him.

CLEMENTINE:
PUPPY LOVE

When we first encountered Clementine, we were so daft with desire for a puppy that we couldn't think straight and we certainly were in no frame of mind to evaluate objectively a candidate for pethood. We had been waiting at least a year for some bitch's happy event that would make us surrogate parents. We were panting for a puppy, eager to smell the sweet fur and milky breath, to admire the silky-skinned full round stomachs after a meal, to caress foot pads so new that they had no calluses. We love little puppies the way some other people fall all over themselves when they see human babies.

No doubt, it was time for us to get one. We had grown into a habit of owning two Bullmastiffs—one youngish, one oldish, one a solid red–coated dog and the other a dark brown striped brindle one. We liked the contrast of the way they looked together, like a regular Kraft caramel alongside the stray chocolate one that sometimes finds its way into the bag. We liked the interaction between the benevolent older dog, lying patiently, well-behaved and housebroken, and the young one, who tugged on its jowls and tumbled playfully around. We were always impressed at how seamlessly older dogs disciplined the young ones, teaching them the dos and don'ts of being a good pet, in effect relieving us of so much of that responsibility.

Minerva, our red Bullmastiff, had lived with Gus, a brindle male, until he died unexpectedly of a heart attack at age ten. Minerva had been an only dog for the last few years. This status suited her perfectly, but not us. The unthinkable idea of a dogless house seemed closer at hand as Minerva aged. A long life span for a Bullmastiff is ten years, and Minerva was already six and a half. We knew that if we waited too long, she would not survive the stress of a new puppy in her life.

Partial blame for our puppymania is owed to the fact that we spent the better part of a year with Mimi Einstein, whose life as a dog breeder and dog show personality we chronicled in our book *Dog Eat Dog*. The book took readers behind the scenes of the show ring, a cauldron bubbling with politics, gossip, and wild displays of ego; in other words, a writer's dream. But even more than the human drama of the show ring, what mesmerized us while writing the book was Mimi's magnificent stud dog, Allstar's Play It Again Sam. We thought him so magnificent that we sometimes stayed up nights imagining what it would be like to own a specimen so glorious. With a thirty-four-inch neck, a gross weight of more than one hundred fifty pounds, and an expression that radiates supreme confidence and strength, Sam is a dog among dogs. We have seen him sit patiently as a four-year-old child he had never before met raucously tugged on his ears, and we have seen one look from his King Kong–sized face send scary-looking men fleeing in the opposite direction. Sam is huge, Sam is gentle, Sam is so sympathetic that he sometimes makes us want to spend fifty minutes every day lying on a couch and telling him our problems. To be with Sam is to know peace.

So when Mimi called around Thanksgiving to let us know that a litter sired by Sam was about to be born, we were elated. This might be a golden opportunity to get our own little piece of doggie greatness. Sam was the father; the mother was another of Mimi's dogs, now owned by another breeder. Champion Allstar's Cover Girl, known as Maxine, lived with Ken and Debbie Vargas of Stonington, Connecticut, where the puppies would be whelped. As an Allstar dog herself, Maxine carried the same wonderful DNA that composed Sam and a host of other beautiful, mellow-tempered Bullmastiffs we had come to know during our time on the show circuit with Mimi.

On an icy day in December we skidded along the highway to Stonington and knocked on the Vargases' front door. Inside all was warm and homey. Big, sweet-faced dogs snored on couches and beds. The house smelled of spicy potpourri and warm apple cider, not of doggie odor and soiled bedding. We had come to the right place. This was a clean proper environment in which to breed a fine dog. Every animal in the house looked content and well fed; there wasn't a trace of the despair and sadness one feels looking at puppies segregated in tiny cages in a pet shop. We had already come to know the Vargases during our time researching *Dog Eat Dog;* and we knew that they had a sterling reputation in the dog world. They seemed to us like perfectionists in everything they did.

Looking around their spotless house, we fairly glowed as we gloated over how we had done everything right. We were model puppy buyers. Unlike the naive amateur who acquires a purebred from a mall pet shop on a whim or finds a bargain puppy through an advertisement in the *Pennysaver,* we had done our homework, and we were certain it would pay off in spades. We knew the breed, we knew the breeder, and we knew this litter's sire: Sam, the greatest dog on earth.

As fools the world over like to say, "What could go wrong?"

Where to Get a Puppy

Buying, Rescuing, Finding,
or Otherwise Acquiring a Baby Dog

Puppy shopping is one of life's joys. It is a time to heft wriggling balls of warm newborn life and watch a scampering litter tumble across the floor chasing toys and each other, then fall asleep, exhausted, in a contented pile. No puppy born is ever anything but cute; to choose one can be a hard decision—a decision of the heart, to be sure, but one that is best made with a clear head, too.

The basic issues are obvious: Big dog or little? An athletic sort or a couch potato? Long- or short-haired? Purebred or mutt? (For some guidelines, refer to The Breed Finder on page 178.) Once you've made up your mind, you then need to decide where to go shopping. There are pros and cons to almost every source of puppies.

BREEDERS

Your decision where to get a puppy may depend on why you want it. If you plan to win blue ribbons in the show ring, you need a purebred, for breed purity is what dog shows are all about. The best place to get one is from a breeder who can sell you a puppy with a pedigree and a family tree of ribbon winners.

Conventional wisdom in the dog fancy as well as literature published by the American Kennel Club decree that everyone should buy a puppy from a breeder. Putting aside the self-interest of those who are in the business of perpetuating purebred dogs, there are many advantages to buying from people who dedicate themselves to a particular breed, most especially if you have your heart set on getting one of that breed. You will be dealing with an expert who can tell you exactly what sort of lifestyle their chosen breed thrives on, what unique needs or quirks it has, and what you can expect at every stage of its life. If you visit the breeder's kennel—which can range from a spare room to a whole separate facility—you can see your potential pet's parents, grandparents, aunts and uncles: all fairly good indicators of what the puppy will grow up to be like. And you can see the environment in which the puppy is raised for its first seven or eight weeks—a crucial time in the development of its personality. As far as that goes, clean and sterile is always good; but it is possible for puppy quarters to be *too* sterile. Like most of us mammals, puppies thrive in an atmosphere of love and warmth, even if it is a little messy; and if you intend for your pet to live as a member of the family, you'll be one step ahead of the game if you can find a puppy that was raised that way.

The term *breeder* can mean many things. It can be a serious dog show pro or a wealthy devotee hobbyist with a climate-controlled kennel and a staff on hand to care meticulously for dozens of animals; it can be a loving enthusiast with one brood bitch and a cardboard litter box in the closet; it can be a nightmarish "puppy factory" where profit is the only motive and puppies are treated no better than a crop of turnips; it can be a young 4-H member who has been encouraged to nurture a litter of puppies in order to experience the reproductive process and learn about nature's ways of parenting, much as farm kids have traditionally done. If you seek an example of breed perfection as the show ring defines it, the best place to find a breeder is a dog show, around the ring where that breed is being shown. Or you can contact a local breed club via the AKC or ARBA (the American Rare Breed Association). Amateur breeders often advertise their litters in the newspaper or on supermarket bulletin boards. Puppy factories do not generally deal directly with the public; they sell their "product" to pet shops via brokers.

When you buy a puppy from a responsible breeder at any level of the game, the deal is seldom *caveat emptor*. Most people who go to the trouble of being midwife to a bitch in whelp want to know how their little ones fare in the world and are happy to offer medical or psychological advice months and even years later. Many breeders we know are so concerned for their bloodline's welfare that they offer an unconditional money-back guarantee: if at any time for any reason you cannot care for the dog, return it to them. We know one such mindful person who received a call from a customer who had bought a dog nine years earlier. The customer was moving to a new home where they felt a dog would be an inconvenience, so they returned their pet of nine years! The breeder received the middle-aged reject with open arms and many misgivings about her poor judgment in selling the dog to this apparently heartless person in the first place.

One of the best things about buying from a veteran breeder is that you are establishing a relationship with someone who has spent years focusing on one breed, and this person likely knows esoteric minutiae about that breed's medical issues that few if any general-practitioner veterinarians can match. For example, before our puppy Clementine was spayed, breeder Mimi Einstein warned us that Bullmastiffs are known among the fancy for having a morbid reaction to a particular anesthetic, although as yet there is no veterinary literature to warn against it.

Some especially rare and valuable purebred dogs are sold with a *breeder's agreement,* by which you, the buyer, agree to let the breeder use your dog X number of times as a stud or (more rarely) as a brood bitch or you agree to let the breeder show the dog until it finishes its championship. The pitfalls of such an agreement are obvious if all you want is a pet to dote over or if you have your own plans that don't include giving away your dog's semen or leasing its womb. If, on the other hand, you yearn to get a taste of breeding and showing, a breeder's agreement can be a good way to start dabbling.

There is a flip-side to buying from a breeder. First, a puppy with real show potential will cost plenty, usually at least a thousand dollars. In most cases the pick of the litter costs even more and will go to people who intend to show it and/or breed it. If all you want is a nice companion dog, you will be paying top dollar for value that has scant bearing on the dog's potential as a good pet.

Buying from a breeder entails the primary pitfall of so many purebred dogs: genetic defects. By definition, a purebred comes from a limited gene pool, and even the soundest breeds have latent flaws that are perpetuated by returning to that gene pool: hip dysplasia among retrievers and shepherds, heart problems among Great Danes and Newfoundlands, Bull Terrier rage syndrome, Dalmatian deafness, Shar Pei eyelid maladies.

Furthermore, many breeders are actively involved in the show ring; and they work hard to emphasize traits of conformation and personality that earn ribbons but do not necessarily make great pet dogs. The "corky" fearlessness that puts a terrier in the winner's circle may not be a welcome trait for a family unwilling or unable to counterbalance their puppy's natural boldness with firm discipline. The vast bulk that earns a Mastiff its championship goes hand in hand with a tendency to develop arthritis and other skeletal ills.

Finally, in buying from breeders you are dealing with self-confessed enthusiasts, people who love a breed so much that they have devoted themselves to it. Dog love, like any other love, can be blind; and rare indeed are the breeders who can forthrightly enumerate all the faults and weaknesses of the dog they love. It is only human for Schipperke fanciers to rhapsodize about the lively, playful, clever personality of the athletic little Skip; they might honestly forget to mention his inbred talent for finding and killing rats or for instinctively trying to herd all members of the family into one room of the house. Bulldog breeders think their beloved sourmugs are beautiful, and while they may warn you about a certain tendency of the breed to drool in hot weather, few will graphically detail how a few summers' worth of Bulldog drool will transform an easy chair's soft upholstery into a repulsive, slimy parchment as tough as dinosaur skin. Every purebred dog has certain qualities that are—let us be kind—not desirable. Breeders are not necessarily the people from whom you'll find these out.

BREED-RESCUE GROUPS

Many national and local breed clubs support "rescue" programs for purebreds. These can range in scope from a volunteer with an extra run or two in a backyard kennel to well-staffed facilities where orphaned, abandoned, and otherwise homeless members of a particular breed are sheltered. A breed-rescue organization can be a great place to get a dog if you have your heart set on a particular breed but don't necessarily want a very young puppy. Most rescued dogs are older because their first home placement simply didn't work out. Therein lies some potential worry—was the dog returned because it was some sort of monster?—but many rescue dogs we've met have been sweet characters who became available only because of human foibles that were no fault of the dogs: divorce, financial problems, a death in the family, or simply the fact that the puppy didn't "show" well enough in the ring.

Breed-rescue organizations usually charge only a nominal fee—they're in it for love, not money—and you will be dealing with people who can tell you volumes about the breed in general and can usually tell you plenty about the particular dog you are getting. The best place to locate a breed-rescue program near you is at the ring of a dog show where that breed is being judged. Someone there will surely know who does rescue work in the area. If you are on-line, go to http://www.akc.org/rescue.htm, a nationwide list of rescue clubs, by breed, maintained by the American Kennel Club.

SHELTERS

Put a gold star on your life's résumé if you adopt a puppy (or an older animal of any species) from a humane shelter. You are most likely saving it from euthanasia—the fate of a majority of unwanted creatures who wind up in shelters—and by extension, you have saved it from a life of misery on the streets or with an owner who abuses it.

Aside from making you glow from having done a good deed, getting a puppy from a shelter has many advantages. First, it is cheap. You will pay a nominal sum, generally less than a hundred dollars, which usually includes basic shots as well as spay or neuter fees; and most pounds and shelters give you a puppy that already has been given at least a quick once-over by a vet. It is not uncommon for the people who staff shelters to be able to tell adopting families a little about their dog: where it was found, if it was part of a litter, and what breed or breeds it seems to be.

Even if the origin of a dog is completely unknown, it is a good idea for the prospective pet owner to make a point of talking to the people who feed and care for the population of the shelter. They are the best resource for getting to know the personalities of their wards. This is important because it can be especially difficult to judge the true character of a dog in a shelter. General chaos—lots of barking, whining, and whimpering—can set an otherwise mellow creature on edge. Some dogs confined for several days may appear more active than they'll be once they get run of the house. And don't be put off by pound newcomers whose ribs you can count. Unless a puppy has developed some sort of chronic health problem, weight lost during its abandonment or abuse by a previous owner can be quickly put back on.

Many people who adopt report that it is perfectly apparent to them that the dog they get *knows* it has been rescued and shows its appreciation by being especially virtuous. Some poor puppies who have spent their early days constantly hungry, cold, and lonely seem to go into a state of rapturous bliss once they are adopted and begin to trust that they will be getting steady meals, a warm bed, and good companionship. They are as grateful as any wretch who comes to realize that heaven is at hand and he is one of its angels . . . and you, the adopting one, are that dog's savior.

On the other hand, there are no guarantees. It is possible the cute little furball you take home from a shelter has ferocious pit-fighting ancestors and as much bloodlust as genes can instill. A warm, loving environment can go a long way to mold a dog's personality, but there are some creatures—of all species—that are born to be bad. To adopt a dog of unknown lineage is to gamble that someday that dog won't suddenly decide to tear the throat out of your house cat . . . or you. Some young strays are so traumatized by their first few terrible days on earth that they never quite get normal. This can be comical—the once-starving foundling who grows up ravenously hungry and develops a figure like Marlon Brando—or it can present real problems to be solved—the beaten pup who cowers in fear at any raised human hand. On a less dramatic note, a young puppy found in a shelter might be adorable at eight weeks but grow into an ugly blockhead by the time it's a year old. If you don't know its antecedents, you cannot be sure what your dog will look like when it grows up, just as there is no predicting its genetically determined personality traits. It is extremely rare to find small breeds or even small mixed breeds in a shelter.

Needless to say, if you are looking for a purebred puppy to show, you will not find it at a shelter. Abandoned and rescued dogs rarely have papers and usually are mutts. But if what you want is a devoted pet with few of the health problems associated with so many of the pure breeds, the selection of a "Heinz 57 Varieties"—also known euphemistically as "The American Breed"—from a shelter just might be a match made in heaven.

PET STORES

Most people who devote themselves to dogs' welfare hate pet shops and advise you never to buy a dog from one. They reason that pet shops exist to make money; and the dogs they sell are mass produced and sold like any other perishable commodity, even ruthlessly disposed of if they go past their "expiration date" and pass out of their cute-puppy stage before being sold.

The rare mom-and-pop store run by kindly animal lovers who get their puppies from responsible local breeders notwithstanding, a majority of the half million puppies sold by pet shops each year come from commercial suppliers, also known as "puppy mills." These are places that produce hundreds of litters per year with no regard for the general health of the breed or the welfare of individual puppies. In his muckraking book *Dog's Best Friend,* Mark Derr described such ill-starred creatures as being "born in squalid, filthy cages . . . and sent for sale at a pet store in the dark back of a hot—or cold—truck, [spending] the most sensitive socialization period in isolation. As a result, they are fearful, prone to aggression and separation anxiety, and largely untrainable."

The fact that a puppy on display in a pet store is "AKC registered" means only that its parents were registered and the proper paperwork was done. Registration is no guarantee of health, temperament, or proper breed conformation. To harsh critics of the purebred dog industry, most of whom endorse interbreeding as a way of strengthening the canine race, AKC registration is a near guarantee of medical troubles down the road: "The AKC has repeatedly ignored the horror of inherited diseases afflicting purebred dogs at an astounding rate," Mark Derr wrote. "Fully one out of four dogs, or 25 percent, from AKC-recognized breeds suffer at least one of the more than 300 genetic disorders identified to date, with the rates among specific breeds running as high as 90 percent for some ailments." (Some pet stores offer guarantees regarding a puppy's good health, but if you have a soft heart there is a terrible danger of bonding with a puppy and not being tough enough to return it even if severe medical problems do arise.)

What about the sympathetic soul who sees a forlorn puppy in a pet shop and longs to give it a good home? For that one puppy, it would no doubt be a good thing to be taken into loving arms. But a realist has to consider that its cage immediately will be filled by yet another hapless product of the puppy industry.

An increasingly popular way to buy a puppy from a pet store is at a store-sponsored "pet fair" to which a local rescue organization brings orphans. This is nice because you won't have to feel any guilt about directly supporting puppy mills; plus you can walk out with a full trousseau.

ON THE STREET

Unplanned puppy parenthood—stumbling across a stray and giving it a home—can be a magical experience. The hazards of this avenue of acquisition are obvious: you can only guess what psychological and physical characteristics your waif will evidence as it grows up and, by definition, you are going to find yourself inconvenienced with the sudden onslaught of caretaking responsibilities.

Most important, let us hope your discovery is not simply a neighbor's dog that has wandered off! The first things any good citizen ought to do after finding a "lost" dog is post notices around the neighborhood, notify local veterinarians, or even place a classified ad in the paper in an attempt to find the owner. What to do if you've bonded with a foundling, then get a call from its original owner—who seems in some significant way unworthy of the new pup—is a moral dilemma to be solved in consultation with Dr. Laura or your clergyman.

PARNELL:
WHERE PERFECT DOGS
ARE MADE

A large part of the Guiding Eyes for the Blind Breeding Center in Patterson, New York, is a kennel where brood bitches look after their young. Imagine a typical dog-boarding facility with cement floors and chain link fencing, but imagine it hospital-clean. To enter the kennel, visitors must stand in a basin in an inch of Clorox to sterilize the bottoms of their shoes; and a large sign warns: VERY IMPOR-TANT! BE SURE TO WASH HANDS WHEN GOING FROM ONE LITTER TO ANOTHER. The warning is signed with a paw print. The kennel smells more like a pleasant hotel than a place where dogs and incontinent puppies live. The floors are washed several times a day; clean newspapers are laid out; blankets changed constantly. Each pen is occupied by a bitch and her litter—usually six to eight pups. In the case of extremely large litters, such as Parnell's, puppies are taken from their natural mother and brought to the pen of another lactating bitch with available teats.

After seven weeks of easy living with its mother, with no job other than to imbibe milk and grow strong, each puppy is brought in from the kennel to the large wood-paneled room used for evaluation. Seven weeks is the ideal time to evaluate a puppy's innate qualities. At this point in its life, it knows nothing of the outside world and has had no training; it is a blank slate, with only its mother's nurturing and its basic nature to guide it through the world. Any earlier than seven weeks, a puppy will have a latent personality, but it will be difficult to read. Later than seven weeks, the environment begins to imprint itself on the young creature and it will be more difficult to separate its basic nature from its learned habits. The tests are designed to measure inborn qualities—confidence, noise reaction, energy level, aptitude.

Despite the rigorous genetic planning that goes into every litter, about one in seven puppies fails the test and is mustered out of the program. There is no problem placing the dogs that fail, because most of them have tremendous pet potential. The breeding center has a list of families eager to get these "rejects." And why not? They have an impeccable family tree and are generally great personalities, but they may have one small flaw that makes them unsuitable for guide work—a slight hearing loss, for instance, or a tendency to ignore or relentlessly explore a novel situation rather than calmly deal with it.

The primary reason puppies fail is known as *worry*—the tendency of a young, bewildered dog to look to humans for a cue as to what to do when the scary umbrella suddenly opens up or when the noisy can is rattled. To the casual pet owner, there is nothing wrong about such a response. It is nice to have a house pet that wants to serve and obey. *Worry* is also a desirable quality in a dog that goes into obedience work, law enforcement, or military service—you want one that instinctively looks to you for leadership and follows your commands without question. But for a service dog, such a personality is all wrong, and may be an insurmountable handicap. A guide dog must be different. It needs a mind of its own; and a seven-week-old puppy who goes through the tests stubborn and hardheaded, unfazed by obstacles and with no overwhelming need for human comfort or approval, is an excellent candidate to continue in the program. Jane Russenberger explains the difference as similar to that between someone who works for a company and someone who runs a company. "A guide dog needs the confidence to take charge."

Those who do pass the test are taken in by volunteers throughout the Northeast who raise them to adulthood. Being a puppy raiser is a noble calling. It requires not only a year and a half of your time and effort, but also an extraordinary emotional generosity, because after spending all that time bringing up the puppy as a member of your family, loving it with all your heart and socializing it as best you can, you must then give it up. It goes back to Guiding Eyes, where professional trainers prepare it for its job, after which it is handed over to a blind person who needs it.

Although Parnell didn't make a perfect score on his puppy evaluation test—a slight tendency toward worry was noted, as was a certain whiney quality when testers stopped pulling the towel across the floor for him to chase—he was impressively curious. And he was self-assured enough to overcome his initial fears of the umbrella and the noisy can full of coins. Between specific tests, the judges noted that Parnell relished poking around the examination room—behind chairs, in nooks and crannies—which was good evidence of a confident, independent nature.

It was decided to allow Parnell to continue his training, but not to neuter him. No potential guide dogs are neutered or spayed at this point in their lives. Those that pass the seven-week test are monitored closely by the staff of the breeding center for the next year and a half in the homes of the puppy raisers. A handful of the truly superior ones—those with superb health and unflappable personalities and family trees of sterling characters—are chosen to be studs or brood bitches, thus making them ineligible for service.

The "family tree" qualification for breeding stock is a significant one. The breeding center keeps detailed records on generations of dogs and selects studs and brood bitches based not only on the individual dog's qualities, but also on evidence of those qualities in the dog's relatives. One spectacular dog in a family of mediocre ones is not likely to pass down its gifts.

If a dog is chosen as a stud for Guiding Eyes for the Blind, removing him from the pool of available guide dogs, he still may go through a full training course at the school so that the staff can observe how well he withstands the pressure of the training (and by extension, how his offspring will stand it). But later, when spayed and neutered dogs graduate and are paired with a blind person, the intact ones go to families in the vicinity of Patterson, New York, where the breeding center can oversee their health and well-being. Every one of these precious animals is given a quarterly medical checkup, including semen analysis for the males. The families that harbor them are expected to clean their ears and clip their nails once a week and to exercise each dog a minimum of three miles every day.

Because it takes several generations and many years to know if a particular stud's offspring, and the offspring of its offspring, carry the qualities of a first-rate guide dog, all of the dogs selected as studs bank their semen starting when they are about a year and a half old. That way, there is always genetic material available from those whose offspring turn out excellent—even if the stud himself starts producing sperm of inferior quality at some point in his life. The Guiding Eyes for the Blind Breeding Center has a complete cryogenics laboratory for freezing and storing the semen in liquid nitrogen, a technique to which they turned out of necessity after the summer of 1995, which was record-breaking hot. Jane Russenberger is a pistol when it comes to assessing sperm motility. "Our poor male dogs got fried that year," she remembers. "Their sperm tails were wrapped around their heads so they couldn't swim. We had to inspect them all to find the motile ones, which meant we could do no natural breeding. At that time, out of necessity, we began a changeover to A.I. [artificial insemination]. Still, fresh is best."

Sex and the Pet Puppy

For too many human beings, the act of spaying a bitch or castrating a young dog is a painful experience. We project ourselves into the canine skin and somehow feel that *our* virility or fertility is being taken away. Poor pup, we hyperbolize: never will she or he hear the patter of little feet or know the pride of parenthood, never will the warmth of canine family life fill the litter box, never will this young and healthy animal know the joy of sex.

It's a crazy way to think about a pet being fixed. (*Fixed:* such a gentle euphemism!) But honestly, who among us doesn't at least occasionally see our dog as an extension of ourselves? Their sex life is our sex life, and few humans are willing to give that up without a fight. The fact is that there are many compelling and virtuous reasons to desex a pet dog.

The average companion dog will be healthier and happier without functioning sex organs and without the compulsion of the raging hormones that control breeding behavior; most dog owners will enjoy their pet more if it isn't horny or in heat; and the world will be a happier place for dogs and for people if fewer dogs are born to wind up unwanted in the cage of an SPCA shelter waiting to be euthanized. Anyone who buys a puppy as a family pet or companion is doing the right thing by fixing it.

A male pet dog can be neutered as young as eight weeks old, but in any case the operation is best done when he is no older than six months, a point at which troublesome macho behavior patterns have not yet been established. Thus altered, a testosterone-reduced male canine will be far less likely to want to "mark" a sofa by peeing on it, will have scant motivation to roam the neighborhood in search of sexual dalliance, won't be eager to pick fights with other male dogs, and probably won't want to bite human beings. If you have any sporting or working plans for your dog, neutering will make him more receptive to learning routine tasks and will eliminate one potentially huge distraction from his working life. All guide dogs, for example, are neutered, the better to concentrate on their job. Furthermore, a neutered male can't get cancer of the testicles (neutering removes them from the scrotum).

A spayed bitch has similar advantages, although the difference in behavior between spayed and intact bitches is not as dramatic as that between castrati and studs. She will be exempt from many fatal uterine diseases, including pyometra and cancer; if spayed before her first heat, she will not develop breast cancer; she won't bleed on the carpet twice yearly when she comes into season: and her scent won't attract relentless packs of horny male dogs. Most important, a spayed bitch will not get pregnant; and an unplanned dog pregnancy can be a stressful, sad, and medically perilous event.

Even a planned pregnancy can be far more than a casual pet owner is ready to cope with. If you have not ever bred a dog before, don't for a minute think it's all fun and motherly warmth and the wonder of new life. Breeding, pregnancy, and whelping demand large amounts of time and money, piles of newspapers and towels, and in many cases (if, for instance, the bitch doesn't have enough milk), willingness to spend weeks of sleepless nights caring for the newborns. Even if all goes well and no puppies die or are born in need of heroic medical care, it is at best a smelly and messy process at the end of which you are responsible for a litter of needy puppies who will have to be placed in good homes. Finding good homes can be difficult . . . unless you're a breeder of champions or are lucky enough to have a currently trendy breed; and if your litter's bloodlines are not of blue ribbon quality (or even if they are), the odds of actually turning a profit are slim to none.

There is one good reason not to spay or neuter a dog: to pass on its genes. Dog shows, the raison d'être of which is to perpetuate the purity of a breed, require that all entrants have functioning sex organs. And it can be argued that if you have a male or female that is a magnificent example of the breed with no significant latent health problems, you are doing a service to the breed to let the Great One procreate. There is a likelihood (but no certainty) that if the right mate is found, the traits that have made this dog so good will be present in its offspring.

CLEMENTINE:
PUPPY DEAREST

Before we were shown the litter of newborn Bullmastiff puppies, we sat with breeder Debbie Vargas on the couch and drank drinks from tall pretty glasses. Our friend Mimi had already told Debbie that we weren't interested in a show dog. What we wanted was a nice brindle female, not to show or to breed, but to love and enjoy strictly as a pet. Out of the litter of eight, there were just two brindles, one male and one female. "Did Mimi tell you the brindle bitch has a white stripe on her face?" Debbie asked with some worry in her voice.

We assured her that we knew all about the stripe, and it didn't bother us in the least. In fact, we thought it might be kind of cute; we liked the idea of some extra detailing.

"She's on the small side," Debbie said sweetly. "But she's my special baby. I have to make sure she gets enough milk and attention. The big ones in the litter are such pushy things, I worry about her all the time." We were moved by Debbie's heartfelt concern.

Debbie could tell we were bursting to see the puppy, so she led us through her sleek modern ranch home with its blond wood trim and light tile floors to the spare bedroom, which despite being plushly carpeted had been transformed into a whelping area. Furniture had been removed to make way for an enclosed pen surrounded by a foot-tall wooden fence. Inside the fence were heaps of shredded newspaper and toys for the puppies to play with when they weren't nursing or snoozing. Above the puppy nest was a radiant heat lamp and among the paper shreds were a few clean terry-cloth towels for cuddling purposes.

It was easy to know which of the puppies was the one we had come to see. She was half the size of anyone else and was lying all by herself at one end of the pen while the seven fine fat ones were piled up atop one another at the other side. The scene reminded us of a high school cafeteria in which the popular kids all hang together while doing their best to distance themselves from the nerd in funny clothes.

"There's my little baby," Debbie said, scooping up the runt in her hands. "Now, you do know that at this age, you can't really tell anything about the way a puppy will turn out?" she said. Mimi had said the exact same words to us that day in an early morning phone call. "They change so much day by day, you just can't know what she'll be like."

She put the puppy on the carpet outside the playpen, then lifted a few of the litter mates out to join her. Although they had not yet mastered walking and stumbled every other step, the big ones began to play vigorously, tumbling over one another on their wrinkled legs, sucking at each other gleefully, and making tiny yelps that were the sound of dogs so young they didn't yet have the physical capacity to bark. But while the others frolicked, the little one wobbled on her four feet, alone in one place. With some clucking and encouragement from Debbie, she began to move, but only in a tight little circle, as if her left front paw were nailed to the floor.

"That's peculiar," we commented.

"Well, she is *different*," Debby replied as we watched the puppy move alone in a pointless circle. Her behavior seemed as inexplicable as that of a character from an Oliver Sacks case study.

When we interrupted her circling by picking her up, she seemed perfectly happy to be held by strange hands. She sucked the ends of our fingers with her wet toothless mouth, and as her little pink tongue lobbed out, we could feel the pronounced ridges on her top palate.

"I think the stripe will fade in time," Debbie said, gazing with dismay upon the shut-eyed little hamster face. "In fact, Mimi thinks it might go away entirely." We nodded politely, although it was hard to imagine such a thing happening, as the stripe now took up one-third of her head and was as bright white as a freshly painted line on an asphalt highway.

Before we left, we told Debbie that we were interested in the pup, but would like to come back in a few weeks for a second look to see how she was developing. In truth we had qualms, some inaudible tone on the tuning fork of caution was humming a silent alert . . .

but an alert to what, we could not say. The puppy was funny-looking but cute, and she enjoyed cuddling with us, which is a good sign. But there was something weird about her that we could not discuss with each other because it was too vague even to put into words. We assumed that in a few weeks whatever it was would either develop and be clearly identifiable or simply disappear.

But the holidays and the pelting icy snows of New England's worst winter in decades made it hard to get back to Stonington, and as we watched the calendar roll by, we kept putting off a return trip. We are not normally procrastinators, and we honestly believed we were eager to acquire a new dog. Were we afraid of what we would see if we went back?

On a particularly grim day at the end of January when ice pellets zinged against the storm windows and wind tore heavy branches off old trees, Mimi placed an urgent call to us. "Debbie is having trouble," she said. "The puppy with the stripe is getting the crap beaten out of her by her litter mates. Sweetpea, the biggest male in the litter, has made it his business to terrorize her. Debbie says that screams from the whelping box are so hideous that she has to rescue the striped one ten times a day."

After hanging up with Mimi, we called Debbie, who confirmed the disturbing report. The runt was indeed having a terrible time. It was a real dilemma because these dogs were only six weeks old. Normally, litters are not broken up until the puppies are at least eight weeks old. It is only two weeks' difference, but those two weeks are vital in a puppy's development. At six weeks old, there is still so much dog-to-dog socialization that ought to be taking place, as well as vital teaching and nurturing from the mother. But none of that good stuff was happening for the runt. Her siblings abused her and her mother ignored her. Her life had become hell. Both Mimi and Debbie agreed that the only thing to do was to remove her from the situation and find her a happy home where she would not be the underdog in an endless gang bang.

"We'll take her," said we in unison without a moment's hesitation. It was the same instinct that made us put money in the Styrofoam cups of unsavory street people and pick up the phone to make a pledge when Jerry Lewis pleaded on the Telethon. It seemed the right thing to do, whether or not we wanted to do it. When we hung up with Debbie, we felt the warm, contented glow again. Not only were we wonderful and responsible puppy buyers. We were kind and humane, too. Oh, we were swell! So swell we wanted to kiss ourselves all over.

We drove to Stonington in a pounding sleet storm. The car was filled with tiny puppy-sized toys, a cozy quilt, and soft towels to bundle her in.

In the whelping room, Debbie had separated the striped-face puppy out from the litter. She was alone outside the pen, standing aimlessly staring at the wall. When she noticed us come in the room, she ran and hid behind a cabinet, her face in the corner and back end aimed in our direction.

Despite our estimable mission of mercy, those distant warning bells started ringing again. Experienced as we were at picking puppies, we were fully aware that cowering in a corner is not a good thing. Puppies should be curious and friendly. Overly shy or fearful puppies can, in time, turn into fear biters, a very bad thing. Furthermore, in the time since we first viewed her, her looks had gotten all the more alarming. We gazed upon the runt's litter mates, their wide wrinkled heads and stalwart expressions, their deep chests and thick legs: these were Bullmastiffs! Had we really waited a year and spent so much time scouting out the consummate gene pool to wind up with a shrunken, cowering, striped-face hamster-dog?

But the deal was done. We paid Debbie with a check and declined a cup of hot coffee for the road. With the little puppy bundled in a blanket, we ran under a barrage of hailstones to the car. The drive home, normally a two-hour trip, took five hours because of the treacherous roads. But by the time we arrived, we had bonded with the tiny little girl. She may not have been beautiful, but she was a very, very good baby. Apparently exhausted from her travails with her siblings, she fell into a deep, calm sleep in Jane's arms. She was quiet and peaceful all the way home.

And then she woke up.

Assessing Puppy Aptitude

A nurturing environment can do wonders to mold a puppy into a dependable adult dog, but nothing can change its fundamental character. As noted in The Breed Finder (p. 178), distinct breeds are known for certain inherent qualities—Bulldog tenacity, German Shepherd fidelity, Poodle wit—and every bloodline within that breed has predictable traits and tendencies. Despite these likely *tendencies,* each puppy is an individual; and the differences in temperament between one Labrador Retriever and another in fact may be greater than the differences between a lab and a Cocker Spaniel.

When shopping for a puppy, purebred or not, the best way to predict what it will be like when it grows up is to meet its parents. Aside from the occasional genetic fluke (like our moonstruck Bullmastiff, Clementine), most dogs inherit a personality that mirrors their kinfolk's. But sometimes, as when adopting from a shelter, there are no parents to meet; and even if you can observe a puppy's whole extended family, every litter has variations in personality—from top dog to runt—that you'll want to know before you pick the one that's right for you.

Beyond meeting the family and visiting a potential pet's childhood home, the most revealing thing to do is to give the puppy a series of prepurchase behavioral tests similar to those performed at the Guiding Eyes for the Blind Breeding Center (pp. 26–30). The tests are not pass/fail, and with the exception of a puppy who demonstrates glaring faults—he wants to kill all humans; he is afraid of anything that moves—they can only hint at the animal's latent personality and suggest in what directions its character will grow.

Before doing the tests, it is important that any potential pet owner reflect on what is wanted in a dog: one that is relentlessly inquisitive or one content to nap through the day? An earnest worker or a clown? A bold hunter or a tender confidant? These tests help predict such qualities. At Guiding Eyes, for instance, they look for signs of a personality that would make a dog especially well suited to a life of leading a blind person, some of which are not necessarily what one wants in a pet—independence, persistence, possessiveness. That is the point of aptitude tests: not to pick the "best" puppy, but the one that fits *your* Perfect Puppy Profile and to determine what, exactly, a dog might best be suited for, whether noble service or simple pethood or something in between.

At seven or eight weeks old, if it has spent those first few months simply being a baby in the company of its litter mates and mother, a puppy's nature will have crystallized, but it won't likely have learned any etiquette and it will have developed few habits, good or bad, that mask its basic disposition. It is the perfect time to appraise its aptitude and personality.

These trials are best performed in a nonthreatening environment where the puppy feels comfortable, but a place freed of extracurricular distractions such as litter mates or a mother, which would naturally command the pup's attention. The tests should take place between mealtimes—you want a puppy that is neither so hungry that it thinks only of food nor so satiated that all it wants to do is nap. Also, your attitude is significant. If you are relaxed and casual and can treat the tests like a gentle game, you eliminate the risk of transmitting your human anxieties to the puppy.

Sociability

With the puppy a few yards away from you on the floor, kneel down facing it and gently clap your hands or quietly cluck or whistle. (Don't make any loud or explosive noises or sudden movements.) A puppy with good friendship potential will be attracted to you and come with a wagging tail and a mixture of curiosity and playfulness. An antisocial puppy will not come or will wander off. An unusually fearful puppy will run into a corner to get away from you. A mean puppy will rush you and try to bite.

Cuddliness

One of the best reasons for owning a dog is to have something warm and nice to stroke whenever you are struck by the yearning for uncomplicated closeness. A cuddly dog can ease your mind and literally lower your blood pressure. But not all dogs are touchy-feely. Test this attribute by getting down on the floor (so your superior size does not intimidate the little fellow). Gently stroke the puppy—don't pat or scratch—while speaking in soothing tones. Don't restrain him in any way. If the puppy stays close and basks in your attention, he will likely grow up to be a cuddlebug. He may roll over, possibly even urinate—both gestures of submission that indicate a willing personality. If the puppy tries to bite aggressively, beware: exploratory mouthing is perfectly normal (but should be discouraged); biting to inflict harm is a bad sign. Any puppy that seems to reject your kindly gestures or cowers in fear may never grow into a warm, friendly sort.

Independence

If you are looking for a pet rather than a service dog, you may not want one that is too independent. On the other hand, no one wants a dog that is servile to the point of groveling. To measure this frame of mind, pet the puppy just long enough for it to feel comfortable with you, then stand up and calmly walk away. A puppy with a good sense of security will follow happily with a wagging tail but not be so desperate for more attention that he whines and gets underfoot. A puppy who refuses to follow or walks the other way will likely grow up with a more autonomous mind-set.

Obedience

In as gentle a manner as possible, roll the puppy on its back and hold it there for up to a minute. Almost every puppy will struggle to a degree, but the one that soon relaxes and is willing to make eye contact with you while it still is restrained has great obedience potential. A puppy that fights relentlessly or stiffens and refuses to look you in the eye will be a tough nut to crack. If the puppy tries to bite you, he could be a major discipline problem; similarly, if he doesn't struggle at all and avoids looking you in the eye, he may not ever be able to develop a close working relationship with a human.

Curiosity

Depending on what you want from a pet, curiosity can be a good or bad thing. If your ideal canine companion lies on the front lawn in a happy daze watching the world go by, you want a puppy with little curiosity. If on the other hand you crave to have a dog join you on vigorous exploratory walks in the wilderness, you'd be happier with a puppy that naturally pokes around to investigate its world. An elementary test is to take a large towel or article of clothing and drag it along the floor, alternating between smooth and jerky movement. How does the puppy react? If he is interested in the unusual moving thing and tags along to investigate, he shows a high degree of curiosity. If he is interested but too afraid to come close, he shows less curiosity. If he runs and hides from it, fear will likely be a dominant feature of his personality. Similarly, if he tries to attack and "kill" the towel, you may have a seriously aggressive character on your hands.

Aural Curiosity

This is a good test also for Dalmatians, a breed in which deafness is a genetic weakness, or for any dog with deaf ancestors. With the puppy facing you, have an assistant somewhere out of the puppy's sight range make a sudden loud noise. (Rattle a can full of coins, for instance.) If the puppy can hear, it will no doubt be startled. Does it run away in panic and cower? Does it quickly recover from being scared, then turn around to investigate? If you are looking for a watchdog, you want one who is very sound-sensitive but not terrorized. If you will be driven crazy by a dog who barks at every car that passes your open window, you should choose a puppy who is less affected by strange sounds.

Ability to Work Well with Humans

If your plans include doing anything with your pet other than hanging around, you'll want one who enjoys interacting with you in games of skill or more serious work activities. These are some ways to test that aptitude:

- Wave a ball or stuffed toy to get the puppy's attention, then throw or roll it a short way across the room. Does the puppy ignore what you've done? If so, it may grow to be a dog who has little interest in interacting with you. Does the puppy run to the object and sniff it curiously? This shows good potential for learning skills to work (or play) in harmony with people. If the puppy picks up the ball and brings it back to you, he's a natural hunting partner. Does the puppy rush to the object and try to kill it? Such aggression, while not necessarily demonic, is best dealt with by expert handlers.

- If the puppy has shown interest in following or retrieving the ball, hold it firmly on the floor with your hand or foot. Does he relentlessly try to get it away from you? Such persistence can be a good quality for an SAR (search-and-rescue) dog and other canines who must perform a task despite obstacles and hardships, but it can be a pain in the neck in a house pet. If the puppy almost immediately loses interest in the ball and wanders off, he might have the makings of a couch potato.

- Test the puppy's attention span by lifting the ball to your face. Make eye contact with the puppy. If the puppy won't look you in the eye or if his attention wanders quickly, he is an independent sort, not likely eager to devote himself to a job of work. If the puppy stays attentive, unafraid to make eye contact, he shows good learning and working potential.

PARNELL:
THE EARLY DAYS

At the age of eight weeks, weighing a mere eight pounds, Parnell left his mother and his litter mates and was taken to New Jersey by Dan and Susan Fisher-Owens, a student couple whose job would be to raise him to adulthood. Parnell was a lucky guy winding up at the Fisher-Owens home: Susan knew just what to do, having raised eleven guide dogs before him, the first when she was ten years old.

Raising a guide dog is a refined and difficult process, usually done by extraordinarily mature teenagers chaperoned by parents under the auspices of the 4-H or a similar service organization. (Curiously, young people have a higher success rate raising guide dogs than do adults in households where there are no kids). Ten years old is generally considered too young, but at the age of ten, Susan was an unusually focused child whose passion to raise and train dogs simply could not be delayed. "When I started I was living in Los Altos, California, and playing on a soccer team coached by a woman who trained guide dogs," Susan recalls. "I read all the books about guide dogs, especially Morris Frank's *First Lady of the Seeing Eye.*" (Published in 1957, Frank's autobiographical story is an account of his life with a German Shepherd bitch named Buddy that he brought back from Switzerland in the 1920s—America's first guide dog. Buddy so changed Frank's life that he went on to found The Seeing Eye in Morristown, New Jersey, to raise and train dogs for other blind people. See appendix, p. 180) Young Susan was inspired by Frank's story as well as by the canine-related work of her soccer coach. She pleaded with her parents to let her raise a puppy for the Guide Dogs for the Blind organization in San Rafael.

"They said, '*No way!*' " she remembers.

But Susan was tenacious. "Let me research it. Let me just find out," she begged. She now explains her strategy this way: "What parent can deny the value of research to a child?" As part of her "research," she managed to get her name on a list of possible puppy raisers, explaining to the people at Guide Dogs for the Blind that by the time her name came up, she would be at least twelve, old enough to take on the responsibility. As it happened, her name came up almost right away. "My parents caved," Susan recalls with just a hint of mischief in her voice, "and the people at Guide Dogs for the Blind, seeing that my family would support me, let me start at ten. On September 18, 1979, I got a black lab female named Florin."

Florin had qualities that suggested she would be a fine guide dog, including a tremendously stubborn personality, manifested primarily in an incorrigible butter-eating fetish. She stole sticks of butter off the kitchen counter, and when Susan and her mother tried to cure her of the habit by booby-trapping quarter sticks of butter with Tabasco sauce inside the sticks, she managed to lick all the butter from the outside and never touch the hot surprise they had put inside. She knew to nab the butter fast, thus avoiding Susan, who lurked behind the counter, armed with a water pistol, waiting to catch her in the act. And she instantly knew the difference between real butter, which was delicious, and margarine, in which she had no interest when Susan and her mom tried to use it as a decoy.

"She turned out to be the toughest dog I ever raised," Susan now recalls. "She was such a challenge because she got into more trouble than any of the others." To the expert trainers at the Guide Dogs for the Blind program, little Susie's reports of Florin's stubbornness were good news. Florin was a born leader. And sure enough, when it came time for Susan to give her up after a year and a half of working with her, Florin went through training with flying colors.

Susan, however, was heartbroken. "I cried and cried and cried when I gave her up," she remembers. "I missed her so much that I couldn't say her name or look at her toys. And the terrible thing was that the day I gave her up, I got a new puppy to train, one named Perky (you know, they come with the names!). Oh, how I hated that puppy! . . . Well, no, I didn't really hate her, but I couldn't stand looking at her because when I did, all I thought of was Florin, whom I had just given away. I swore then and there that once I got rid of Perky I would never get another. That was it, the end, all over. It was simply too emotionally draining to be with a dog so intensely for a year and a half, then let it go.

"But something happened when Florin graduated after her training. At the formal ceremony during which she was handed to her new owner, I watched a blind woman shuffle to the podium awkwardly, groping her way. I saw her take Florin's harness and stand up tall. I saw her smile. I saw her walk away, proud and confident. That dog of mine that had been so incorrigible and so crazy could make such a difference for someone who really needed her. I knew what she had been to me, but at that moment I saw what she could be to someone else. And that hooked me forever. My mother and I did ten more dogs in California."

After Dan and Susan were married, they raised a dog together in Chicago, where they had moved for Dan to work on a Ph.D. This dog, named Ewell, came from an organization called Canine Companions for Independence, which prepares dogs to serve people with physical handicaps beyond blindness (see appendix, p. 185). In addition to basic training and socialization, Dan and Susan taught Ewell to fetch and to drop items at their feet or in their lap. They taught him to tug on things when asked, a precursor to opening doors for someone unable to do so on their own; and they taught him to jump into a lap and sit calmly, a skill useful for working with someone in a wheelchair.

After Ewell was trained and placed, Dan and Susan Fisher-Owens moved to New Jersey and brought Parnell into their home in July, 1995, during the record-breaking heat wave. Within a few days of living with him and starting on one of their first tasks as puppy raisers—housebreaking—they came to believe that he would never make it as a guide dog. Parnell preferred having "accidents" on the floor of their home to going outside where he was supposed to relieve himself. They wondered: was he so afraid of the outdoors? Or was he so stupid that he couldn't understand the basic rule that elimination should be done al fresco? In either case, they grew mighty worried. When they did take the little puppy out, he dug in his heels, he flopped down in the driveway, and he sprinted for home as soon as he thought he had the chance. He didn't even want to play or explore the neighborhood as any ordinary puppy would do.

The Fisher-Owenses were stumped. To help them solve so fundamental a dilemma, they enlisted Matthew, a ten-year-old yellow lab who now lived with them as a pet. Matthew had been a guide dog, raised by Susie in California. He had led a life of distinction, attending the signing of the Americans with Disabilities Act in Washington, DC, with his owner, a blind lobbyist. When the owner died, Matthew went back to Susan to live out his golden years. Parnell delighted in the company of the older dog indoors and frequently slept curled up in the big blond's warmth. But as soon as they went out, Parnell slumped. Even with Matthew in the lead, the tiny puppy showed little interest in sniffing his way along fragrant streets and stopping at nice big trees in the park or bright red fire hydrants. All he wanted to do was go back inside the house, where he could piddle and make his BMs in all the wrong places.

When even Matthew started trailing after the puppy toward the front door to get in the house, it dawned on Dan and Susan what was going on. "Parnell was smarter than we thought," Susan says. "It was sweltering that summer and our house was air-conditioned. He quickly learned that going outside meant getting hot. He preferred being scolded for his accidents inside to baking in the hundred-degree sun." Fortunately for Parnell, the Fisher-Owenses soon happened to move to a home without air-conditioning. There, the headstrong puppy instantly decided he loved going for walks, especially in the early-evening breeze. And by the time he was a year old, temperature simply was no longer an issue—an important development for a dog that someday might find himself assigned to work for a master who lived in Tucson, Terlingua, or Atlanta.

Curriculum for Puppy Guide Dogs

Most dogs turned over to blind people by Guide Dogs for the Blind of San Rafael, California, have been raised by 4-H Club members who join "puppy clubs" in which they share the joy, insights, and tribulations of transforming a twelve-week-old puppy into a well-behaved adult dog ready for formal training.

Puppy raisers receive their dog already inoculated against distemper, hepatitis, leptospirosis, parainfluenza, and canine parvo-virus, and it will have been dewormed; but it is the youngsters' responsibility to bring their wards in for rabies shots at the age of four months. For those who live near enough Guide Dogs for the Blind in San Rafael to bring the dog to the campus, all veterinary care is done on-site and all expenses are taken care of. Outside veterinary care, as well as food, toys, and travel expenses, are paid for by the puppy-raising family.

Beyond maintaining the puppies' good health, the primary responsibility of a puppy raiser is to mold the dog's personality to make it suitable for the life ahead. "Only puppies raised in a loving family environment with opportunities to learn about the outside world have any chance of becoming Guide Dogs," the organization states.

A loving environment is only the start, for raising a guide dog demands more hard work than anyone devotes to raising a pet. For two years, the dog undergoes a rigorous course of home schooling that demands not only the attention of the puppy raiser and the puppy raiser's family, but care and caution from friends, neighbors, and anyone else with whom the dog-in-training develops a relationship. Guide Dogs for the Blind puts it this way: "Raising a puppy requires time, money, energy and a generous heart. The puppy you decide to raise today may become someone else's Guide Dog in the future. You will have all the hard work of house training and socializing the puppy. You will be the one with the chewed-up slippers and soiled carpets. Your love and teaching will enable the puppy to grow into a well-rounded, happy dog."

Specifically, these are the things a puppy needs to learn:

- The desire to please and be with humans, wanting praise and attention.
- How to behave properly at any time, even in situations that encourage distraction and play.
- How to be comfortable in as many different environments as possible, ranging from busy city walks to residential and country walks.
- How to allow themselves to be easily groomed and cared for, without moving around and resisting being handled.
- How to avoid any physical behavior that would be harmful to a blind handler, such as jumping up.
- How to be relaxed and obedient when traveling on all kinds of transportation.
- How to be a healthy eater of a common, nationally obtainable dog food, maintaining proper body weight and healthy coat without exceptional supplements and care.
- How to be friendly and relaxed around other animals without seeking their company and attention more than that of human companionship.
- How to be friendly and relaxed around all types of people.
- How to calmly and confidently negotiate all types of stairs, surfaces, and elevators.

In order to develop all these admirable traits, puppy raisers need to expose their dog to:

- All varieties of people (strangers and friends) as obstacles and distractions, touching and talking to them while they are trying to work.

- Food temptation on floors, on tables, and offered by people while they are trying to work.
- Many types of animals distracting and approaching them while trying to work.
- Having to concentrate on work around heavy traffic, crowds of people, playing children, people playing games with other people and with other dogs.
- Traveling on all types of transportation: buses, cars, trains, planes, subways, etc.
- Working around and past unusual-looking and -acting people.
- Working around a variety of noises present in everyday life.
- Behaving in every public situation.
- Remaining calm while crowds of people clap and scream.
- Confidently yet cautiously negotiating all types of stairs, surfaces, and elevators.

Clementine:

Dogs Behaving Badly

One way we rationalized choosing a tiny, frightened runt from a litter of otherwise exemplary Bullmastiffs was to take into consideration the personality of Minerva, our older dog. Minerva herself was a very timid soul. As a puppy, she required only a raised eyebrow to stop any bad behavior. The word *no,* spoken with just a hint of anger or threat, was enough to make her flee in terror. She wanted nothing more than to do the right thing. The very thought that we were unhappy with something she had done sent her into a sulking depression. She was so easy to be around—no problems at all, eager to please.

Even in the prime of her youth, Minerva was no great show ring beauty; and now as she eased into old age she had grown big and goofy-looking with too much loose, wobbly skin hanging from her old body and a peanut-sized head with a bony point at the top that made her look like Walt Disney's Pluto. In her dotage she had begun to remind us of the character actress Marion Lorne, who specialized in playing flibbertigibbet old ladies in 1950s movies. On occasion, Jane would hang her good opera-length pearls around Minerva's neck and we would admire how good they looked on this canine dowager.

Because of her sensitive nature, Minerva had suffered to some degree in the company of Gus, our big brindle male. He frightened her, not because he was mean but because he exuded top-dog karma. He was undeniably king of all animals. He always had first dibs at the water dish, a new toy, or the better bed. When he died we could almost hear Minerva breathe a sigh of relief. The skin rash that had plagued her all her life miraculously cleared up. She discovered the joy of sleeping on the rug in the spot closest to the fireplace where Gus had always made his camp. She now bedded down each night at the foot of our bed—the best place in any house for a pet dog to claim. Minerva spent two blissful years as an only dog. Now we figured that at her advancing age, she shouldn't have to cope with some strutting, bossy puppy pushing her around. Perhaps the fainthearted runt would be a perfect match for someone of her delicate nature.

But the moment we brought the new puppy through the door of our home and unwrapped her from her swaddles of blankets, we knew we had underestimated the intensity of Minerva's insecurities. The mere sight of the puppy made her teeth start to chatter, like those windup joke dentures you buy at a novelty store. She didn't come around for a sniff, she didn't study the new creature that we set down on the floor in front of her, she didn't back off and wait to see what it would do. She turned around and ran as fast as her arthritic bandy legs would carry her, up the staircase to the landing. The puppy was still too small to climb stairs, so Minerva was safe. And there Minerva stayed, staring down in fear and trepidation as if a little white-striped gremlin had suddenly invaded the house.

The landing became Minerva's safe place. From it, she could peer through the banister at what had been, only a few days before, her happy world. She stayed there a week, and when it was time to eat, drink, or go out for a walk, we served as her bodyguards, escorting her through the house and making ourselves human barriers between her and the horrifying, hand-sized puppy.

According to news reports, our small Connecticut town got more snow that winter than Fargo, North Dakota. One time, the snowfall was so deep we actually were trapped in the house for two days, unable to open the door until the town road crew dug us out. The bad weather gave us much time to sit inside and contemplate the strange effects visited on our household by the arrival of the six-week-old Bullmastiff.

With the exception of Minerva's impending nervous breakdown, the puppy's first few days at home were fairly easy. She spent most of the time sleeping; and when she was awake, she was perfectly content to lie in our arms and be cuddled. She was so impossibly tiny and defenseless. We cradled her like a newborn baby; Jane held her to her chest so she could feel a maternal heartbeat. We talked soothingly into the tiny brown earflaps, we rubbed the smooth toe pads and toyed with the little wagging tail. Michael crooned her name, Clementine, which we had chosen to honor a favorite John Ford western. Whether or not they will be campaigned in the show ring, all Allstar dogs get names to honor real or fictional celebrities. With that in mind, her AKC papers listed her as Allstar's Darling Clementine.

We called Mimi every morning to report on the puppy. When we hung up with Mimi we called Debby Vargas and repeated the same stories. Clementine had no shortage of concerned godmothers and expert advice.

Gradually, her sleepy calm gave way to curiosity, and after three days she began to explore the house with verve. This was always the case with puppies, a development that Mimi confirmed: "They do wake up once they know where they are," she chuckled.

Removed from the dreaded Sweetpea and the rest of her big, bumptious litter mates, Clementine's timidity quickly faded. And compared to the confines of the whelping box with its simple furnishings of newspaper and towels, our house was a sensory bonanza, filled with the smells of dogs from decades back, and the tangle of present scents. There were closets with laundry baskets of aromatic garments, there were bathtub ledges lined with shampoo bottles waiting to be pushed over by a curious nose, and bedspreads to be tugged on. Best of all, there was a talking, squawking green Amazon parrot named Lewis who exuded a perfume all her own that smelled like clover honey.

Clementine had found her Wonderland. Watching a puppy discover a new world is one of the joys of the dog-owning experience. It can be fun to see one come strutting proudly into the room dragging some old sweatshirt they discovered in a closet; and although mildly exasperating, their ceaseless curiosity about anything pokeable, pushable, tuggable, or chewable is also an exhilarating expression of youthful joie de vivre. But there was something different about the way this puppy explored. Or maybe there was just more of it. All the puppies we had known enjoyed periods of intense play, then fell into equally intense sleep. The odd thing was that Clementine appeared never to sleep. She was relentless. Instead of wearing her out, her playfulness only stoked her up for more play. And that amplified her need to sprint madly up and down the hallways until one of us physically intervened to try to calm her down.

As a breed, Bullmastiffs are not high-energy characters. Sometimes they can be positively sluglike, a personality that perfectly fits our own rather laid-back natures. It is not uncommon for Minerva to spend six hours straight snoring on the couch, until one of us pokes her and gets her to get up for a walk or a meal. One reason we wanted an offspring of Mimi's dog Sam is that Sam is especially serene, even for a Bullmastiff. When he is resting peacefully on his ottoman at home, nothing disturbs him. Even when he visits a new strange place, he is content to sit and watch the world go by with the haughty curiosity of a regal potentate. That's what we like in a dog: calm. We would never intentionally choose a breed that needed a ten-mile hike each morning or hours of Frisbee play in order to relax. The very word *bouncy* makes us uncomfortable.

But apparently Clementine never read the breed standard as to what a Bullmastiff personality should be. After a week with her, we began to suspect that her father was not Sam but the Energizer Bunny. Even though she was more torqued up than we had expected, we were still fully confident of our ability to turn her into a well-adjusted dog. We planned on raising Clementine with the same tried-and-true methods we had used on all our others.

The first task was to introduce Clementine to the concept of eliminating outside instead of in the house. Housebreaking is an easy, logical process. We had always depended on the use of a crate to accomplish this task. Crating a dog is a good and common method because dogs are reluctant to soil their own nests; plus a crate allows the owner to get some sleep or a time-out without having to worry about what the puppy is getting into. From the basement we dragged up the big metal dog crate—a sturdy thing, if a bit battle-scarred from having serviced the needs of many previous puppies, including four Bullmastiffs, an English Bulldog, and a Bull Terrier. We padded it down with clean towels and newspaper on the floor and we added a toy or two for mental comfort. We placed the crate in the hallway right outside our bedroom in order to monitor what was going on.

The first night can be one of the worst times of owning a new puppy. Upset by their recent separation from family of origin, many of them whimper, yell, and cry when they are left alone as they have never been in their short lives. These sounds are sorrowful enough to melt the coldest heart, but every puppy-raising expert agrees that the worst thing you can do is take the puppy out of its bed and cuddle it until it stops whining. Such misguided kindness simply teaches a puppy to whine—a lesson learned quickly and then unlearned only with great difficulty. And no one likes a dog that is a whiner. So we listened to her mewl as we lay in bed with our eyes wide open and prayed for her to relax.

After an hour of listening to Clementine moan, we peeked round the corner to make sure she hadn't gotten herself tangled or injured in the crate. She was fine, but it was a wrenching sight. She looked so impossibly small and scared, dwarfed by a plush owl toy and a squishy magenta platypus. We walked back to bed, and lay there unable to sleep, wondering if we were doing the right thing, wondering how we could be so cruel to a scared six-week-old puppy.

Usually a whimpering puppy wears itself out after a few hours and falls asleep. If you are lucky the puppy falls into a deep sleep. And if you are diligent, you will get up early enough to wake it before it relieves itself in the crate, at which point you immediately take it outdoors for a walk, teaching it where to do its business. When it goes outside, you praise it to the sky. A few days of this and *voilà!* Housebreaking 101 is over and done with. Most dogs quickly catch on to this routine, not just because they enjoy the praise; it's their nature to want to keep their bed clean. That's the point of crating.

Again, Clementine hadn't read the book about how to be house-broken easily. She whined all night and we resisted getting her out of the crate, lest we inadvertently train her to whine for attention. But at 4:30 A.M., when finally we felt it time to rescue her and swoop her outside to do her business in the proper place, we got to the cage and found it filled with her waste. Not only had she soiled her bedding; she had rolled in it, and dragged it all over the crate, squishing her stools through the bars of the crate onto the hallway rug. The horrid scene reminded us of angry convicts in maximum security prisons who throw shit at the guards out of rage.

"Big deal." We shrugged. It takes some puppies a while to be able to control their bowels and bladders. So we cleaned the cage with Lysol and washed the owl and platypus and scrubbed the rug. We used paper towels, soap, and water to try to freshen Clementine so she didn't stink. At that moment, we felt terribly sorry for her, imagining how traumatic it must be to be taken away from Debbie's home, brought to a new place, left in a metal cage all alone, lie in shit and pee all night and not get any sleep. We were about to cry at the injustice of being a puppy, but Clementine was busy squirming out of our arms. Ready to start a day of play, she seemed quite unconcerned about her frightful night.

The first week or two Clementine lived under the flag of puppy immunity, too young to be held accountable for any misdeeds. By the time she was ten weeks old she had still not spent one night in her crate without soiling it repeatedly and had never settled into the idea that she should be in the crate in the first place. She barked and howled all night long, taking only fifteen-minute breaks to nap. Like many new parents of human babies, we forgot what it was like to sleep through the night. Our nerves were growing raw.

"Do you think she has to go out?" we croaked in bleary voices to each other at 3 A.M., after having cleaned the smelly crate only a few hours before.

"I'll check," one of us volunteered and staggered into the hall. We would open the crate, to Clementine's delight. She wiggled with glee at the sight of us, and when we picked her up she licked our faces like we were long-lost friends.

At 3 A.M. she was an interesting armful because at least half the time she was covered with fresh feces she had rolled in. We would wake up fast, clean her and the cage, then ourselves, then place her back in it only to have her start yipping for our company again.

If by some miracle the cage was clean when we opened the door, we picked her up in our arms and ran her outside to the frozen grass of our lawn. There, she did nothing but stare up at us with huge round eyes the size of silver dollars. We stood in our bathrobes until our teeth chattered and her little puppy body shivered. "Go!" we implored to no effect. We carried her back inside, and once in her warm crate, she happily did what we had urged.

By the time she was three months old her toy platypus had been washed so many times in hot water and Clorox it looked like it had been skinned alive.

Each night we lay side by side together in the darkness thinking guilty hateful thoughts about the puppy in the hallway. "Why doesn't she shut up?" Michael said.

"I don't know, but I can't stand it," Jane moaned.

We went down the litany of possible things we had omitted. Yes, she was walked; yes, she did her business before she was crated; yes, she had toys and fresh bedding; yes, we put the radio on softly so she could hear it; yes, there was a night-light in the hall; no, she didn't eat anything weird before bedtime.

The answer that eluded us then now seems perfectly apparent. Clementine thought it was great fun to be taken out of the crate and brought downstairs a few times a night, no matter how unfun we tried to make these wee-hour expeditions. She steadfastly refused to do anything at all outside except run around and play, saving her bowel explosions until she was safely back in her cage. The puppy had succeeded quite well in training us to take her out of the cage in the middle of the night. We had trained her not one iota.

As Clementine grew, so did her boundless energy. Once she was fed her breakfast, the first order of the day was to locate Minerva, who was still camped out on the landing of the staircase. When she was no more than ten weeks old, we watched with amazement as Clementine placed the top half of her little V-shaped body on the bottom stair and used all the strength in her rubbery puppy front legs to pull herself up onto the step. Working methodically and with tireless persistence, she then pulled herself to the second stair. We reached back in our memories for other puppies who attempted to climb these same steps. Most didn't even try until they were much older the she. We watched in astonishment as Clementine was already up to the fifth step and climbing higher. Minerva, who had been observing the process from the landing with wide-rimmed, disbelieving eyes, stood up and bounded six more steps to the top of the staircase. We grabbed Clementine and brought her downstairs to play with a toy. We knew that in only a few days Minerva would be hers.

Of course all Clementine had in mind was to play, and Minerva, too gentle for her own good, was part of the problematical equation. She was incapable of doing what senior dogs normally do in this type of situation, which is to issue one good growl, raise their hackles, and send the puppy fleeing for safety. Instead, Minerva lay on her side like a beached whale, a look of utter panic on her face as Clementine gnawed on her with her sharp little teeth. The big old dog waited helplessly until we came along to unhook the puppy. She then got up and scampered away. To protect Minerva, we erected a gate at the foot of the stairs. We would open it and let her run up the stairs to safety, then close it before Clementine could follow. This frustrated Clementine tremendously, causing her to paw at the gate and bark and yelp at Minerva until we picked her up and carried her to another room in hope something else would divert her attention.

In an attempt to focus her energy on something other than Minerva, we cleaned out the pet shops and mail order catalogs for things to play with. Within a few weeks Clementine had amassed a wealth of soft chewy ropes, Nylabones, rubber ducks, rawhide bones, a chewable fishing pole, a squeaky pork chop, a cloth Frisbee, a plastic Frisbee, tennis balls, and chewy slices trimmed from cows' hooves. Our friends Victor and Tina brought us a huge basket of hand-me-down toys of which their dogs had grown tired. But no toy was of interest to Clementine. She would sniff a toy, feign interest for ten seconds, then ignore it, preferring to scout out Minerva, or even worse, Lewis our parrot for some finely focused harassment.

Lewis is housed in a large floor-standing cage in the den, where we watch television and enjoy our morning coffee and bagels. Like an expensive restaurant chicken, she is free-ranging; we keep the cage door unlocked when we are home and she is used to strolling about as she pleases. (Lewis, we should mention, is a female; she got her name because we thought she was a male for the first six years we owned her. By the time DNA blood tests revealed otherwise, it was too late to rename her.) In her eleven years with us, Lewis has seen so many dogs that she has no fear of them. In fact, dogs are afraid of her. Although she weighs just over a pound, she is a study in avian machisma. Like many parrots, she is a larger-than-life presence with a loud, commanding voice and an attitude of utter fearlessness, underlined when necessary by a great flurry of snapping spread wings, whistles, and beak swoops like a swordsman with a rapier. She has proven herself capable of sending the biggest Bullmastiffs scampering away with one good beak-strike to the spongy black surface of a curious nose.

Lewis and the dogs had always gotten along splendidly. Many of them allowed her to walk over their reclining bodies as if they were fur-covered mountain ranges. Sometimes she would climb onto Gus's back and he would buck around the house like a rodeo bull while she held on with her skinny long gray toes, whooping with glee. Sometimes Lewis would resort to dirty tricks to scare the dogs. She would yell, "No!" or "Bad dog" in her perfectly replicated imitation of our voices and bamboozle a dog into stopping whatever it was doing. We kept Lewis away from Clementine the first few weeks we owned her, believing Clementine still too tender to meet the real dominatrix of the Stern household.

But by Clementine's twelfth week, we were at the point in our relationship with her that such fine issues of etiquette seemed irrelevant. We were simply trying hard to hold on to what was left of our normal daily routines. Our sleep was disturbed and so was our work. Our offices are in our home, so there was no getting away from her demands. One of us had to watch her at all times to make sure she wasn't getting into trouble. If we placed her in the crate during the day she would bark like crazy, which made writing difficult if not impossible.

We desperately attempted to hold on to our morning ritual, which brought us together in the den for coffee and bagels and watching the news on TV. There is a comfy dog bed in the den, not too far from the bird cage, where Minerva likes to lie, and we added a second bed next to it, hoping that Clementine would imitate her elder. One day we walked into the room balancing breakfasts in our hands, the dogs tagging along behind us. Minerva went to her familiar spot and lay down. Clementine pounced on top of her like she was a trampoline. We separated them. We showed Clementine the bed we hoped she would come to call her own. Jane attempted to get her to lie down by lying on the bed with her and making noises of delight. When Jane got up so did Clementine. The coffee was growing cold. "Let her walk around, she will settle down," Michael suggested optimistically. We sat down and clicked on the TV set. By this point, Minerva had fled the room, leaving Clementine alone with us and Lewis.

We hoped she would be lured by a choice of two squishy round beds but instead she decided to pace, one of her favorite activities. This was a dog who never seemed to walk but moved with a demented gait that we had seen in the feline houses of zoos with too small cages. Like a lion or leopard or some other predator in bondage, Clementine circled and circled, following her own footsteps like she had when she was two weeks old, except now her eyes were wide open and hungry for action. She seemed intent on going nowhere fast.

Lewis had been observing the scene from the top of her standing floor cage. She skittered down the manzanita wood perch to the apron of the cage where she could get a closer look. At this height she and Clementine were eye-to-eye. We hesitated to intervene because we had seen similar dog-bird encounters countless times; and it seemed best to let the two animals work out their relationship with each other with us monitoring but not interfering unless necessary. One good swipe from her beak was Lewis's efficient way of making sure that a dog never bothered her again. As Clementine leaned close, Lewis issued a robust "Hello!" and started whistling a snatch of her favorite tune, the theme from *The Andy Griffith Show.* It seemed an avian peace offering. We could see Clementine inhale the honeyed parrot scent that Lewis exudes when she is excited. The stand-off suddenly broke when, to our horror, Clementine launched herself toward Lewis in a full airborne attack, her sharp white teeth clicking like castanets in her broad pink maw. No slouch herself, and recognizing superior force, Lewis flew straight upward like a helicopter in fast retreat.

"NO!" we screamed in unison, jumping from our chairs and pulling Clementine away from the cage. Instead of looking ashamed or frightened, she looked quite pleased with herself. She could now put another notch on her gun belt. She had scared the hell out of Minerva, and now she had Lewis on the run. This was some strange behavior for a runt, we thought.

The next morning we took our places in the den, coffee in hand. Lewis was reluctant to slide down to dog-eye level. She sulked at the top of her cage, keeping one paranoid eye out for the puppy. She could not even be lured down for her customary piece of Jane's bagel.

Clementine was Johnny on the spot. She had learned quickly that the big birdcage was the source of excitement and she began her grand rounds circling it. "Stop that!" we yelled at her, stomping our feet and clapping our hands to get her attention. All the noise and action only made the game more fun for Clementine. She apparently thought it was some sort of organized family scream or tribal dance where the point was to make as much noise as possible. She upped the tempo, finally ending the cage-circling with a surprise double back flip toward Lewis that crashed her instead into Jane, who was on her feet attempting to make a grab for Clementine's collar. The collision sent a mug of hot coffee down Jane's freshly laundered shirt. "I hate her," Jane wailed, and ran upstairs to the bedroom in tears.

By the end of the week our calm morning ritual had been transformed into a nerve-shattering contest of wills—a contest we were losing. Our voices were hoarse from shrieking at Clementine, to whom "No!" had become less an admonition than a theme song. Not content to annoy Minerva or Lewis she began to see fun possibilities in other aspects of the den. She methodically pulled art books off shelves, she gnawed firewood into splinters, she separated the speaker cover from the TV and the wires from the VCR. Needless to say, any shoe or boot left on the floor was fair game; blankets on chairs, hems on curtains and remote controls made a tasty snack. Anytime we pulled her off anything, she quickly discovered something more dangerous or destructive.

Desperately in need of time out from her exhausting antics, we decided to put her in a circular exercise pen, a five-foot-wide metal-wire enclosure we obtained via emergency overnight delivery from a dog supply catalog. The "ex-pen" was placed in our kitchen, far enough from the den so the barking protests would be somewhat muffled. The pen had been Mimi's suggestion. Like most breeders she does not cotton to the idea of puppies running about unsupervised. Professional dog people in general do not share the romantic notion that dogs should always run freely about, unless perhaps you happen to have 2,500 private acres of Montana wilderness as your backyard. In most cases running free is the shortest route for your dog to wind up in your neighbor's yard or under the wheels of a passing car, and within the home, an unattended puppy will wind up in the garbage can, gnawing a live electrical cord, or eating a box of laundry soap. Crates or holding pens are a great idea and have saved many a puppy's life and many an owner's sanity.

Clementine went peaceably enough into her new pen, which like the smaller crate contained blankets and toys galore. And with high hopes, we went upstairs to our offices. There we would spend the morning productively thinking, conferring, and writing.

Hardly any time had passed before we heard an awful clanking and thudding accompanied by strident yelps and barks. We ignored it, or at least tried to. The barking and yelping grew louder. Finally, we walked to the stairs and gazed down. There we found our Clementine, still inside her pen. But like a baby Hercules she had managed to walk the five-foot metal structure that surrounded her all the way through the kitchen, down the hallway, and up a few steps of the staircase.

We forgot about trying to get any work done that morning and instead went to the hardware store for big steel bolts that we used to tether the ex-pen to the kitchen wall and floor.

Stages of Puppy Life

Different breeds mature at dramatically different rates, and the old chestnut about one dog year equaling seven human years is totally misleading in terms of mental and physical development. At one year old most dogs have reached sexual maturity and are well into adolescence; and at two they are adults. Some of the large breeds are geriatric cases by the time they are seven; conversely, it's not unusual to meet a robust Chihuahua of seventeen or eighteen. Nevertheless, most puppies share a common growth curve, which is extremely valuable to know if you have one. Here are the basic stages, followed by a timeline of puppy development.

Weeks 1–6: Babyhood

A puppy needs its litter mates and its mother and little else. After three weeks, when its eyes and ears open, it begins to develop basic motor skills and canine-to-canine sociability. Within litters, individual personalities begin to develop: top dog, one of the pack, shunned runt. While it is a good thing during this phase for a puppy to come into daily contact with the kind hands of a comforting human (as preparation for its future life), it is from peers that it learns what it needs to know. Puppies can be weaned at about four weeks old (although most mothers' milk lasts to six or seven weeks), and by the fifth week, they should be capable of eating from a dish.

Weeks 7–10: The Blank Slate

A crucial stage in a puppy's life, and generally its first extended exposure to human society. During these two to three weeks, a puppy that is well cared for, nurtured, disciplined (in only general and benevolent ways), and finally welcomed into a "family pack" of humans has a very good chance of growing up to be a fine canine citizen. Generally, no puppy should be separated from its litter earlier than the age of eight weeks.

Aside from plenty of love and patience, the most useful tool a human can have starting at about the eighth week of puppy development (and beyond) is a crate. Make the crate, as Martha Stewart might call it, *a good thing* for a good dog. Never put the puppy in it as punishment. Do what you can to make it his special place—comfortable and warm, with a favorite soft toy or two. He will quickly learn not to soil there and always have a happy refuge you can send him to when he is a pest. Dogs of all ages need a secure place of their own, even if it is just a mat in the corner of the room.

The most important thing a puppy learns during this phase is its name. Say it often, but take care never to associate it with harsh words or punishment. Every time you catch the dog looking at you, say its name in as sweet a tone as you can muster.

A puppy that is abused during this stage of development or— even worse—neglected or isolated will have a hard time ever learning to be comfortable or dependable. Alas, it is during these weeks that most "puppy mill" product is transported from farm to pet shop.

Many trainers recommend introducing secure and agreeable puppies to a leash when they first come into the home at eight weeks old, simply by letting them drag it along (with supervision, of course). But no puppy of this age should be given a harsh correction with a choke chain or pulled on a leash: its bones are still too delicate.

Weeks 11–16: Adolescence

It is during this stage of development that a puppy begins to use logic and good sense (one hopes!). With a responsible owner guiding it along the right path, it learns its name, it learns to be housebroken, it learns to walk on a leash, it figures out such basic home routines as bedtime, not chewing shoes, and where its special place is. Elementary obedience work can be started at this time, but most three-month-old puppies have a short attention span, and whatever lessons are taught should seem more like play to them than work. During this phase, the word *no,* spoken as severely as possible, should be imprinted in the puppy's mind as a cue to instantly stop whatever it is doing and pay attention. The crucial element here is timing. Five seconds after some bad behavior is too late; "*NO!*" is effective only if it interrupts the bad thing the puppy is doing. In other words, it is of no use whatsoever to scold a dog if you find a pillow it chewed up hours earlier or a stain on the rug where it piddled the night before.

At twelve weeks and up, a puppy can be enrolled in kindergarten class to develop elementary socialization skills and learn the fundamentals of good behavior. During this period, call the puppy by name in a cheerful tone of voice, repeating the name and praising it warmly when it comes to you. In an area with no distractions, let the puppy tag along after you, saying its name often and bending down every few minutes to give it a friendly pat. Walk in a straight line, then a circle, then more complex patterns, and let it follow you. This can lay a great foundation for more complex interaction during the next phase of learning; and it at least teaches the puppy to pay attention when its name is called.

Weeks 17–24: Basic Training

With the fundamentals of good behavior already under its belt, a four-month-old juvenile canine is ready to really master sit, stay, come, and heel even under trying circumstances; and he is ready to tackle more complex skills. Still, a half-year-old is not yet ready for anything that requires a finely developed intellect, mature patience, or extended focus. Serious training for any of the vocational skills will come after six months. Under six months, it is still best to make training take the form of play, with plenty of time for frolic and fun between lessons.

Six Months to One Year

For most puppies, this is an awkward time similar to the teen years in humans. Different parts of the body seem to grow at different rates. A dog will suddenly become tall and gangly, or its body will mature at a quicker rate than its head. Similarly, mental development happens in fits and starts; and for the first time, an apt puppy will show its ability to learn complex behaviors and to put its canine logic to good use perfecting such skills as tracking, retrieving, obedience, and agility. Although most dogs can begin serious, formal training in their chosen field at six months, the trainer must expect a two-steps-forward-one-step back progression. It is in this adolescent phase that unfixed male dogs will begin to lift their legs to urinate, thus "marking" territory and expressing their malehood. Female dogs will come into their first heat. Traditionally, females have been spayed and males neutered at about six months; but many vets believe that the operations can be performed as early as eight or twelve weeks.

After One Year

Almost every breed of dog is considered fully developed at one year old, but many of the larger breeds neither fill out physically nor reach a mature psychological plateau until the age of two. Guide dogs, for example, are not specifically trained for their job until they are twenty months old. Fanciers of schutzhund (a sport in which dogs demonstrate their skills at tracking, obedience, and protection work) say that although a willing puppy may start training at six months old, it is not uncommon for it to need two years to attain its Schutzhund I title. Our own misbegotten Bullmastiff Clementine could not be left alone, uncrated, until she was eighteen months old, which is about the time she finally completed the transformation from a pitiful runt into a lusciously muscled (albeit pint-size) bitch.

THE FIRST EIGHT WEEKS TIMELINE

Please remember that, like human babies, no two puppies develop exactly alike; and the difference between breeds can be dramatic. Still, this timeline is a good general reference for when puppies do what:

Week 1: A healthy puppy will crawl and suck, but its mother's licking is needed to encourage elimination.

Week 2: Eyes open.

Week 3: Ears open, tails begin to wag, tentative barking sounds are made. Puppies begin playing with each other and defecating without encouragement from mother.

Week 4: Baby teeth appear and many puppies take tentative first steps. Weaning may begin and solid food gradually introduced.

Week 5: Puppies begin to enjoy exploring their world and can become smitten with human companions. Given the chance, a precocious puppy will figure out how to eliminate away from the place it plays and sleeps.

Week 6: The litter has become a pack in which each puppy has a place in the hierarchy. Top dogs command first licks at the best teats or dishes of food; the runt and underdog must settle for sloppy seconds.

Week 7: Mother's milk dries up (although most breeders prefer to wean puppies a few weeks before this).

Week 8: A puppy's individual personality will have taken shape and most will have the psychological strength to part from their mother and litter mates and go out into the world. Even some of the toughest will whimper their first night or two alone. The company of another dog is the best way to alleviate separation anxiety, but sometimes a trick as simple as a ticking alarm clock wrapped in a blanket (reminding the pup of its mother's heartbeat) will provide solace.

Parnell:

The College Year

When Parnell was not quite one year old, in the spring of 1996, Susan Fisher-Owens went to Johns Hopkins University in Baltimore for an advanced degree in public health. She took Parnell with her. Guide dogs in training such as young Parnell are not covered by the Americans with Disabilities Act, which mandates allowing service dogs in places pets cannot go; but in Baltimore, thanks to Susan's persuasiveness and good people in authority at Johns Hopkins, Parnell went just about everywhere. He was in classrooms, the hospital, the medical school, and the public health buildings. He rode buses around the city and became a well-known character on campus. At graduation time, Susan's classmates voted Parnell the Student Most Likely to Go Into a Life of Public Service. However, Susan notes, he never did get an actual award. She explains: "The reasoning was that he hadn't paid any tuition or fees."

It is the job of a puppy raiser to expose potential guide dogs to the widest array of situations, from fireworks displays and busy city streets to long periods of inactivity and quiet at home. All the crowded halls and classrooms Parnell encountered during his tenure at Johns Hopkins were the best kind of basic training for a guide whose duties might someday include leading a person with a very active life.

Sailor: Daddy of All Guide Dogs

Twelve years old, eighty pounds, coal black with hypnotic dark eyes and a cool nose, Sailor is the most prolific stud Guiding Eyes has ever known. He is the Babe Ruth of sires: begetter of 44 litters totaling 338 puppies, 35 of which went on themselves to become breeding dogs and 179 of which went into service as guide dogs for the blind.

Sailor was born Beechcrofts C'Brook Seaworthy on February 9, 1985, son of Champion LoBuffs Seafaring Banner and Ch. Beechcrofts Skylark; and he spent the early years of his life in the show ring, where he became a champion. But Sailor's true allure had little to do with good looks. His was a presence that transcended proper conformation. Confident and willing, strong but gentle, this was a male Labrador Retriever to make an astute breeder of service dogs weak in the knees at the thought of the splendid progeny his testes might generate. With the blessings of his owner, Diane Pilbin, the young dog was put on a Guiding Eyes brood bitch.

Sailor's puppies showed much promise, but it was not until two years after they were born that another breeding was attempted. Breeding program director Jane Russenberger needed that time to be certain that Sailor's offspring would mature, train, and work without developing any physical or mental flaws that might have been recessive in their father. The pups turned into beautiful adults and went on to lead the blind, so more breedings were done with a range of bitches. Retired from the show ring, Sailor became Guiding Eyes' leading stud. He went to live with a family in Connecticut who brought him to the breeding center several times a year for health check-ups, for social visits with a staff who grew to adore him, and to deliver his fecund seed.

Retired from stud service now for two years, Sailor returns to the breeding center often, whenever his human family travels. It is an occasion anticipated by Jane Russenberger and the staff with joy; and for us, one such visit was a rare opportunity to meet a canine saint.

When we arrive at the breeding center one crisp autumn morning, we find the honored guest stretched out across a central hallway in the office area of the converted home in such a way that no one can go anywhere without gingerly stepping over him. "That's the way he likes it," Jane Russenberger says, looking down at the sleepy black lab, who has a salt-and-pepper muzzle and a set of somewhat shriveled—but still intact—testicles that hang to knee level. "Sailor likes to be where everybody has to step over or around him." At the mention of his name, Sailor lifts his head a few inches off the floor and opens one eye to see what's up. His tail thumps a few times, he stretches his legs in the luxurious manner of a man of leisure, and he gradually gets to his feet. Although his coat is glossy black and his eyes are clear as crystal (and examined yearly by a canine ophthalmologist), his gait, stiffened by arthritis, reveals the pains of advancing age. When Jane Russenberger says, "Let's go talk in my office," Sailor seems perfectly to understand her words, just the way a human colleague would hear them, and so he toddles right along to find a nice place on the floor in the office where he can relax, rest his chin on a visitor's shoe, and be part of the conference, which is, after all, about him.

For those of us who know dogs mostly as sybaritic emotional sponges, always eager for attention and affection, it is stunning to become aware of this creature's extraordinary poise, so unlike a mere pet. "A noble dog!" Jane exclaims. "Secure, and yet willing. As a stud, always ready but never really wild. A classy kind of guy."

Of course, Sailor himself never served as a guide dog. What is truly significant about him, therefore, is not the fact that he possesses all the sterling qualities of character and physical soundness that guide dog trainers seek, but that he passes them on to his children and his children's children. "His kids do reflect him," Jane says, telling us that trainers are always thrilled to get a Sailor pup. She points to a candid photo in a collage on her desk in which Sailor is lying with his front feet crossed, looking relaxed. "His puppies even lie down just like he does, with their legs crossed. Like him, they live long, they have few health problems, and they all have that easygoing confidence." She pauses to gaze upon him with the kind of awe you might see in the eyes of a symphony conductor admiring a prodigy. "But not one of his children is even half of what he is," she concludes. "We have never created a dog quite like Sailor and I doubt we ever will."

"Thank you, I think we know what we need to know," one of us says, winding up the interview. At these words, which he understands as clearly as if he were raised speaking English as a first language, Sailor rises from the floor. He shuffles toward our chairs so he can dot the back of our hands with his cool, wet nose to say farewell. On his own, he exits the office and heads through the hallway into the kitchen where the breeding center staff have gathered around a small table to eat sandwiches and to chat about some seven-week-old puppy tests scheduled for the afternoon. He joins the social group around the table, tail wagging and eyes gleaming, a big pink-tongued smile on his face. His business meeting concluded, Sailor is happy to spend lunch hour among a group of nice human friends he has known through the best years of his good life.

CLEMENTINE:
PUPPY KINDERGARTEN

When Clementine was twelve weeks old, we enrolled her in a basic obedience class, known as puppy kindergarten. This was something we had done with many previous puppies, and it always was a big help getting them well behaved and properly socialized. Twelve weeks was a month sooner than we usually started our puppies in training, but she had had all her shots against communicable diseases . . . and we were desperate.

Not surprisingly, she was the youngest dog in the class, and the smallest, despite being a Bullmastiff. She was dwarfed by zaftig six-month-old labs and Golden Retrievers. The instructor worried that she might be too young, might not have enough attention span to keep up with her classmates, but agreed to let us see what happened.

To our amazement, Clementine proved to be an A student. She quickly mastered the sit, the stay, and the down. When it came time to go through her paces, she was all business, focused like a laser beam on the task at hand. She didn't make a single mistake, and while other puppy parents had to come to class with rolls of paper towels for cleaning up accidents, Clementine didn't once think of peeing or pooping on the gymnasium floor. The kindergarten teacher declared her a genius and asked the other people in the class to study her and learn from her. "She is perfect," we were told; and we accepted the accolades feeling like great impostors. We tried to explain to the instructor that she was out of control at home, but were met by disbelieving stares and suggestions that we stringently follow the same commands at home that we did in the classroom.

We did, and she didn't. Home was not class and she knew it.

There is a truth about taking a dog to obedience class. It is like going to the hair salon and coming home looking gorgeous, then the next day you try to do it yourself and your hair looks weird and by the end of the week your great new "do" is a disaster.

In class Clementine was the model student. She sat, she heeled on cue, she stayed stock-still while Michael walked twenty feet away and then came bounding to his feet when he called her from across the room. We had been to enough obedience classes to know that you have to work the drill at home, too, for the training to work; and at home, on the leash, Clementine was flawless. But unclip the leash and she was a different dog. She would not do a thing we said. Our plans did not include being leashed to a dog for the rest of our lives.

A basic tool of dog obedience training is a choke collar—a thin metal link collar that you snap tight for moment around the dog's neck when it misbehaves or goes in the wrong direction. This is called a "correction," and it is done by making a fast tug at the leash, creating an instantaneous tighten-and-release effect on the dog's neck. In the hands of a novice, especially a klutzy novice, a choke chain can be a tool of torture, for the point of it is not to actually choke the dog but just to startle it. Michael, Clementine's handler in class, is relatively proficient with a choke chain; and it took only one or two quick corrections for her to understand any command. Once she understood, she obeyed, and needed no further corrections.

When teaching a dog to obey, your voice is the most important tool you have. "No" must be said with sharp authority, and all those in the class who shrieked it desperately or whispered it failed to communicate the proper expression of control to their dog. Saying no correctly is one of the hardest things to master. One man in class was a source of great anxiety for the near hysterical teacher as she watched him tighten the collar, bellow "NO" with theatrical panache, but then forget to release the collar. His poor dog was being strangled right there in front of all of us. Michael and the dog choker were the only men in the class; the rest were suburban ladies who had a lighter touch with the choke chain, but also too light a touch with the word no.

The obedience class proved to us that Clementine's problems had nothing to do with a lack of intelligence. She was fully capable of understanding commands and executing them. Clearly, based on all the little gold stars she had won in kindergarten, she was no dope. She had the ability to be a good dog, but not the desire.

By the time class was over Clementine was five and a half months old and still was not housebroken. We had changed her diet, thinking the food she was on might be contributing to the problem. We checked her for worms, we checked her for bladder infections, and at the suggestion of Debbie Vargas we mail-ordered a special organic dry kibble that cost a small fortune. Her other annoying habits had not gotten any better either. She barked all night in her crate and when she was out of it during the day she was destructive around the house, aggressive with Lewis, and aggravating to Minerva.

"How's the puppy?" Mimi asked over the phone one day.

"Oh, fine." We lied.

Long silence. What could we say? That we hate this dog, that she is ruining our lives? After all, we had spent a year begging Mimi for a puppy. And this wasn't just any puppy. This was a daughter of Sam, who we all agreed was the world's most perfect animal.

Clementine was changing our long-held belief system about children and dogs. In the past when we had encountered a badly behaved puppy or kid we jumped to one conclusion: there is something seriously wrong with the way the dog or youngster is being raised. But where did that leave us and Clementine? We honestly believed we had done everything right, at least we did everything the way we had done with our other dogs, who were delightful to share a home with. If someone else told us this story, we would just naturally assume they were terrible puppy parents. Were we?

And so we kept trying. Perhaps exercise was the key to calming down her hyperactivity. She simply never grew tired and never rested. Michael took to walking her for miles every morning. Michael, who is fit enough to have recently completed a triathlon, returned home limp as a rag, ready for a nap. Clementine, invigorated by the forced march, was panting with glee, eager to find some new household mischief. Later that day she ate the latigos on our horses' show saddles, which we kept on display stands in the living room. We had sprayed them with Bitter Apple, a bitter but nontoxic product designed to discourage dogs from chewing; but we concluded that Bitter Apple was her favorite condiment.

We observed her closely. Our obsession with figuring out her strange behavior had taken precedence over work, as well as over any kind of normal life. In her ceaseless energy and impunity, she seemed to be in her own world. With her eyes as round and bright as the headlights on an old DeSoto, nothing intruded on her awful inner-directed scheme of chaos and anarchy. Her endless pacing never ceased, and was soon accompanied by an even more alarming habit. She would latch on to the hem of Jane's skirt, trying to provoke a tug of war. Jane would yell at her, clap her hands, rattle something, shoot her right between the eyes with a water pistol (a suggestion of many trainers for dealing with a mischievous puppy caught in the act of doing something bad), even give her a whack on the rear end. But the gleam in Clementine's eyes only grew brighter with all the obstacles and danger, and she grabbed onto Jane's clothes even more vigorously. The game stopped only when she was removed by physically unclasping her jaws and carrying her to the ex-pen for lock-down. There she barked for hours at the indignity of it all.

From her insecure beginnings Clementine had developed into a dog that was immune to all the usual intimidation tactics. This confounded us because we were veterans at puppy one-upmanship. No dog we had ever owned had ignored us the way Clementine did. Unless she was on the leash, with the choke chain on, the word *no* meant absolutely nothing to her. With all the other puppies we had raised, eye contact and a sharply spoken *"No!"* were all that was necessary to put a rebellious soul back on the straight and narrow.

All the previous dogs we had owned came with a superego. They may not have understood all the fine points of right and wrong, but once they were taught the difference, they seemed to want to do the right thing. They had the ability to look at a chewed corner of a rug, remember the punishment they received, and not want to repeat the crime again. Clementine was missing that basic mind-set. She was a walking id, a creature of unbridled desire who seemed to live every moment as if there were no moment before it and no consequences. Every day was the first day of creation for her, and all the on-leash corrections and explicit *nos* seemed to erase themselves like a magnetized cassette tape. Her mind was as fresh and clean and blank every evening as it had been that morning. We began to wonder if she might literally not be hearing us. Could she be deaf? We took her for an examination at the vets and yes, she could hear perfectly well.

Her problem was not physical. In fact, for a runt she was growing at an admirable pace. At eight months old, she broke the one-hundred-pound mark, healthy in every measurable respect.

We continued to rack our minds for a solution to Clementine's behavior. We remembered that in the late 1970s on assignment for *Yankee* magazine, we traveled to upstate New York and spent some time with the monks of New Skete, a Russian Orthodox order that is famous for its dog-training abilities, and for the classic dog-training book *How to Be Your Dog's Best Friend.*

At the monastery, Brother Job explained to us that dogs are pack animals. Like their wild brethren the wolves, they naturally establish a hierarchy with whatever creatures they share living space. Even the most domesticated dog sees life from this perspective; and so it is the job of every dog owner to establish a position as the leader of the pack, or in canine behavioral terms, the "alpha wolf."

We took our well-worn copy of the monks' book down from the shelf and reviewed it. It seemed to us that we had done all the important things correctly. We had disciplined Clementine like a top wolf to a bottom wolf. We had rolled her on her back and held her with one hand at her throat until she stopped squirming. We had grabbed her by the sides of her face and glowered in her eyes until she averted hers. We had given her a sharp smack under the chin (coming from below, such a smack won't make a dog hand shy), but to no avail. No matter what her crime and its immediate punishment, she shrugged it off a few seconds later and her mind was again free of inhibitions.

We knew we needed outside help, but we were hesitant to open the yellow pages and pick a trainer. We had done that years before, with deep regrets. Our problem back then was a somewhat recalcitrant Bull Terrier. Given the stubborn nature of the breed, we thought it would be a good idea to get started early with some professional help. We found an advertisement of a training service that promised to turn our dog into Rin-Tin-Tin overnight. The trainer who came to our house was a tall, skinny Ichabod Crane in a black leather motorcycle jacket and with a lupine expression on his face. He took one look at the slit-eyed puppy he was supposed to work with and went back to his car for heavy-duty equipment.

We were smart enough to intervene when he walked toward the dog with a choke chain that had spikes pointing inward in one hand and a long rope noose in the other. He explained that his strategy was to hang our dog from a big branch of the tree until it stopped struggling and learned "who was boss." By the time the Better Business Bureau and the Humane Society investigated, he had left town and probably set up shop in another state. Anyone can call himself a dog trainer.

Vocations and Hobbies: Skills Dogs Can Learn

Most puppy purchasers want nothing more than a friendly four-legged companion; but the pleasure of raising a young dog to adulthood can be deeply enriched by work beyond the basic-training skills of *sit, stay, heel,* and *come.* Focused activity for play and pleasure is also a wonderful way for a dog to learn that discipline can be fun.

The range of activities a dog can master in order to enjoy itself or to do service are enormous, from the acquisition of lethal attack strategies to learning how to fake a talent for adding two plus two. Some inbred talents can be hard on the dog, not to mention demanding of an owner: just because you own a Malamute with the muscle and grit to pull a sled doesn't necessarily mean your dog—or you—will be happy exposed to the grueling and sometimes fatal physical hardships of running the Iditarod from Anchorage to Nome, Alaska; and owning a hale Pit Bull is no excuse for engaging in the cruel sport of dog fighting. Still, experts in canine behavior universally agree that dogs are happiest when they can, in some way, fulfill their genetic destiny. As is true of so many people, even if indolence comes easy a dog will thrive if it has things to do other than laze around the house.

Whether you've got a Bloodhound who loves to track an intriguing aroma or a pointer with a natural talent for bird-watching, it is a special pleasure to help your dog develop its innate abilities. What a marvel it is to watch a young Border Collie's instincts rise to the task when he first confronts a flock of sheep; it is sheer joy to ride with a pack of callow hounds enthusiastically cubbing across the countryside in search of an alluring scent. There is something especially gratifying about owning a pet who really contributes to society, such as a search-and-rescue dog who can be called from home in an emergency (like a volunteer fireman) when a child is lost in the woods. And on a less exalted note, who doesn't enjoy the tell-tail wag of a show-off pet dog that has been trained to fall over and play dead when you pretend to shoot him with a toy pistol?

Beyond the skills that will be learned, formal training is a wonderful way to bond with a puppy because it gives dog and owner a common interest and ensures that time spent together isn't boring. The specific type of training you choose will depend to a large degree on the puppy's nature and instinctive talents. Only big breeds have the strength to do rescue work; retrievers, needless to say, learn hunting skills more readily than do lapdogs; Poodles make poor attack dogs, just as a Rottweiler won't likely do well as a merry sidekick for an acrobatic circus clown. But almost any dog can benefit from almost any training, even if the breed and skill do not exactly match. Our Bullmastiff Clementine does terrific agility work, although at 120 pounds of dense muscle and heavy bone, she could never compete on the level of lean and lithe animals that dominate the sport's upper echelons. Still, the agility course is an excellent focus for her boundless energy. It seduces her into enjoying what was always so difficult for her, which was to concentrate on a task at hand. And it gives us a welcome opportunity to do what we found so few occasions to do during her early, aimless puppyhood, which is to praise her.

While it is possible to send a dog off to a trainer or to have a trainer come to your house to do the work, such a plan leaves out all the fun—and hard work—that a master and puppy can share. Furthermore, what the dog usually learns in such instances is to pay close attention *to the trainer,* and unless the trainer also trains you very well to mimic his cues, commands, and attitude, and unless you diligently apply what he has taught you, the dog may quickly forget everything it has learned and lapse into the sybaritic lethargy of so many jobless pets.

This raises the issue of how best to bring up a puppy if you are a busy person who spends significant amounts of time away from the house—and from the dog who lives there. People who work long hours and don't have a Significant Other to care for a pet all that time will need to find dog walkers and house-sitters who can tend not only to the puppy's physical need to go outside frequently, but also to its psychological need for guidance and companionship. In lieu of a responsible and caring stand-in to assume such responsibilities, the person who will be away from home most of the time is better off acquiring an older, steadier dog that doesn't require the constant attention puppies need to grow up happy and healthy. If lack of time is a big concern, logic also dictates that homebody dogs—toys and some of the non-sporting breeds—would be a better match than athletic sorts that thrive on hours of exercise.

The first order of business for *any* puppy, whether destined for a great career or not, is puppy kindergarten, starting at about twelve weeks old. A veterinarian or local breed club can tell you where and when kindergarten sessions take place. They help the dog learn to socialize politely with other dogs as well as with other people and they teach such fundamentals as sit, stay, heel, and come. Like human kindergartens, schools for puppies vary considerably in approach. Some are fairly strict; others are just fun. To know if a class seems right for you and your puppy, try observing a session or two; or talk to people whose puppies have graduated.

The following are some of the basic curricula you and a puppy can undertake once the fundamentals have been mastered in kindergarten. In cases where no contact information is given, the best source about where and when to learn about and/or compete in these activities is the American Kennel Club at 5580 Centerview Drive, Raleigh, NC 27606, (919) 233-3600 or (919) 233-9767, or e-mail: info@akc.org. The monthly *AKC Gazette* is a regular source of purebred-dog information supplemented by an events calendar with specific listings of dog sporting events.

Dog Shows

Showing a dog in an AKC-sanctioned show demands no specific displays of skill because such shows are beauty contests. Nevertheless, a successful show ring dog is one who has been trained by a handler to exhibit his best features in a charismatic way. In addition to proper breed conformation, a certain degree of natural extroversion is necessary as a starting point; beyond that, handlers train show dogs to pose in the handsomest possible posture when the judge inspects them and to circle around the ring with brio. The very best show dogs, like theatrical hams who steal the show, thrive on the applause of an audience and might even learn to divert attention from any competitor who is attracting the judge's eye.

Canine Good Citizen

This is a program sponsored by the AKC in which pet dogs get certified as worthy members of society. This is fun stuff if you don't have high ambitions to win trophies and ribbons or compete in athletic events, but nonetheless want to do some constructive work with a young dog to improve its quality of life (and the quality of life of all the people who know it). Canine Good Citizen courses, administered by local kennel clubs, 4-H Clubs, and private dog-training facilities, help puppies learn these ten basic skills:

1. Accept a friendly stranger: no barking, no shying away.
2. Sit calmly to be petted.
3. Stand politely to be groomed or examined by a veterinarian or other caregiver.
4. Walk on a loose leash. A test not as strict as "heeling," walking nicely in this case simply means no tugging or dragging behind.
5. Navigate a crowd. Can a dog go past and around people without undue sniffing or fear behavior?
6. Sit and down on command. Will a dog stay in one place while the handler moves to a point twenty feet away?
7. Come when called.
8. Behave pleasantly around another dog. A little sniffing and tail wagging is fine, but no aggression is permitted.

9. Calmness in the face of distractions. Can a dog handle a passing jogger, a dropped bag of groceries, a car backfire without abject panic?
10. Separation without anxiety. If you leave your dog alone or with a stranger, will he sit calmly? Barking, whining, and panic are not allowed.

Obedience

Like graduate school after matriculation in a program of sit-stay-come-heel, obedience training teaches a dog to heel off the leash, retrieve things on command, make a broad jump, sit still off-leash for long periods of time, and remain lying down for extended periods when the handler walks away. Obedience titles include CD (companion dog), CDX (companion dog excellent), and UD (utility dog). Breed purity or conformation is not an issue in obedience trials: any dog who is mentally and physically fit can compete.

Agility

The gymnastics of the canine world. Dogs are trained to navigate up, over, and around hurdles and jumps at top speed with minimal cues from a handler, i.e. off-leash and frequently at some distance. Obstacles include a teeter-totter, a closed tunnel, a single-bar jump, a double-bar jump, and an A-frame ramp. The AKC sanctions the NA title (novice agility), OA (open agility), AX (agility excellent) and MX (master agility excellent). The United States Dog Agility Association has titles that range from AD (Agility Dog) to AAD (Advanced Agility Dog) and MAD (Master Agility Dog). As in obedience testing, breed purity is irrelevant.

Hunting

Konrad Lorenz speculates that the bond between humans and canines originally was formed as a hunting partnership when wild packs of jackals learned to trail after unclothed bands of *homo sapiens* hunter-gatherers—feeding on their refuse and helping them bring larger animals to bay. This companionship and interdependence of hunter and dog now has special meaning to many nature lovers who train dogs to hunt and go afield with them as a welcome antidote for too much civilization. To a great number of wing shooters, the joy of the hunt is less in killing birds than in working closely with expertly trained pointers and retrievers who have the opportunity to ply finely honed talents for flushing and finding their quarry. Conservationists note that using a retriever is the epitome of efficient game management: virtually all wounded and killed birds wind up in the game bag rather than lost in field or lake.

If you don't want to actually hunt game, but have a dog whose natural aptitude is as a hunter, many breed clubs stage field trials in which you and the dog can work together to bring out his best and earn the titles of Junior Hunter, Senior Hunter, and Master Hunter. Competitions include trials for beagling, pointing, retrieving, and flushing.

Herding

Breed clubs around the country stage noncompetitive clinics and tests to measure the instinct of your dog to control a flock of ducks or a herd of sheep, cattle, or goats. It isn't only the traditional herding breeds that have a natural gift for this sport; but it is especially amazing to see an untrained Collie or Shepherd draw on its genetic legacy to hold and move a group of animals. If your dog does have the ability, it can be great fun to enter herding trials in which dogs compete both against a standard and each other. Herding is done under the direction of a handler, for which you get to hold a long wooden staff—a tool of the trade unchanged since the Bible was written.

Lure Coursing

Do you have a young Rhodesian Ridgeback, Basenji, Greyhound, Afghan, Borzoi, Pharaoh Hound, Irish Wolfhound, Scottish Deerhound, Saluki, or Whippet? If so, you already know that your dog cannot resist chasing things. It's the nature of these breeds. Lure coursing, in which many breed clubs offer noncompetitive clinics, is a wonderful opportunity to give the fleet-footed sight hounds an opportunity to do what they do best. Lure coursing competition, which measures speed, agility, and endurance, sends dogs after a mechanical lure that moves along a set course on an open field. Canines with a natural bent for this kind of chase simply adore the activity; and it is a great way to keep them fit, mentally as well as physically.

Earthdog

Small terriers have traditionally loved to "go to ground" in search of quarry. Earthdog trials assay this talent in AKC-registered terriers and Dachshunds, who are placed at a den in which a pair of adult rats have been secreted. The rats are held safe in a cage so the little dogs don't get to kill them—as instinct would dictate—but the dog that gets to the quarry fastest wins. Titles that can be earned are Junior Earthdog, Senior Earthdog, and Master Earthdog.

Schutzhund

Schutzhund (meaning "protection dog") was developed in Germany at the turn of the century as a three-part dog aptitude test to measure potential for police and military work; now it is a spectacular display of how precisely canine instinct can be harnessed to serve human will. The first talent measured is tracking ability: can a dog follow a scent over mixed terrain—and, if conditions allow, in inclement weather? At advanced levels of schutzhund competition, scents are laid by people the dog has never sniffed, a full hour before the dog is sent to ground. Secondly, a dog must demonstrate its ability to sit, stand, stay, heel, and retrieve even when distracted by flailing arms, screams, and gunfire. The final test is protection. Dogs are trained to attack on command and to stop attacking on command. This looks scary, but in fact a well-trained schutzhund dog, absolutely in tune with its handler, shows no aggressive personality traits until the moment it is ordered to attack, i.e. their ferocity is nothing personal. The United Schutzhund Clubs of America notes that, "All bites during the protection phase are expected to be firmly placed on the padded sleeve and stopped on command and/or when the decoy discontinues the fight. The protection tests are intended to assure that the dog is neither a coward nor a criminal menace."

Schutzhund requires a tremendous amount of mental acuity and physical prowess (on the dog's part) and a lot of time in training with a handler. Puppies start when they are about six months old.

For information, contact: United Schutzhund Clubs of America, 3810 Paule Avenue, St. Louis, MO 63125-1718, (314)638-9686.

SAR

A puppy that is strong, eager to please (but not clingy), relentlessly curious, and very well socialized may have search-and-rescue potential. Generally, large (but not giant) working dogs with thick coats are those that succeed in this field, for it can demand much physical exertion, agility, and the ability to withstand severe weather. While many SAR dogs are permanent members of police and fire departments, a majority live in private homes and perform their service alongside their master/handler: when someone is lost, after disasters in the wilderness, when a building collapses and victims are trapped inside. Black Paws, a Montana-based international organization of owners of SAR Newfoundlands, lists the following qualifications among its requirements for membership:

- The dog must be a purebred Newfoundland.
- The handler must hold current certification in CPR and basic First Aid.
- The dog must not be attack-trained.
- The handler shall be responsible for keeping his dog safe throughout search missions and protect his dog against known hazards. Whenever possible, the handler will put his dog's needs ahead of his own during and after search missions.
- The dog team shall function well on land or water, and be able to negotiate and maneuver in the various terrain and geographical conditions prevalent in the chapter's region, whether moderate, rough, or extreme. The team shall also work in various weather conditions.
- The dog shall be able to locate lost victims in a given search sector with a reliable, readable "alert" and "refind" under favorable conditions and in a reasonable amount of time. The dog team will work in water, woodland, avalanche, and disaster situations and subject to experience, discriminate between live and dead victims.
- Dog teams will cooperate fully with law enforcement and other agencies.
- Dogs are trained for helicopter and aircraft transport.
- Some Black Paws chapters offer advanced expertise in additional areas such as diving, mountaineering, skiing, medical assistance, and man tracking. Teams are prepared for overnights unsupported depending on conditions and are prepared to search for a full-time shift. Dogs are trained to "air scent" without a scent article.

For information about Black Paws in particular, contact: Susie Foley, PO Box 365, West Glacier, MT 59936, (406)387-4225.

For information about SAR in general, contact: National Association for Search and Rescue, 4500 Southgate Place, Suite 100, Chantilly, VA 20151-1714. Phone: (703)222-6277; fax: (703)222-6283; e-mail: info@nasar.org.

Also: The American Rescue Dog Association, P.O. Box 151, Chester, NY 10918.

Frisbee

In the 1970s, a hound named Ashley Whippet became a TV sports superstar demonstrating an amazing ability to chase after a Frisbee, leap high into the air, and nab it mid-flight. Today, Frisbee-tossing can be observed in almost any city park and is organized as dog-versus-dog competition in many locations, involving catch-and-retrieve, distance tests, and freestyle Frisbee tossing set to music.

Naturally, certain breeds are better suited to Frisbee catching: sight hounds and retrievers, whose predisposition is to go after game, are naturals; but most dogs of almost any nonphlegmatic breed enjoy a good game of catch. It is easy to test whether or not your puppy has an aptitude. Simply roll a Frisbee across the ground. If the pup is interested and goes after it, he likely has the makings of a Frisbee athlete, airborne or not. To find out more about detailed training and competitions held throughout the year, contact National Capital Air Canines, which sponsors instructional clinics in the DC area. They can be reached at 2830 Meadow Lane Falls Church, VA 22042, (703)532-0709 or (703)K93-DISC, or via e-mail: ncac@discdog.com.

Flyball

A team sport for seriously athletic dogs and owners who want to devote copious amounts of time to coaching a four-dog team. Developed in California in the 1970s and demonstrated on the *Tonight Show,* Flyball is a relay race over a forty-foot, four-hurdle course that starts when a dog steps on a launcher and sets a tennis ball flying. The dog catches the ball and leaps over the hurdles, to and fro, at which point the next dog goes and does the same thing. All this happens lightning fast—the world record is 16.7 seconds. Dogs can earn titles from FD (Flyball Dog) to FMCh (Flyball Master Champion). For information, contact the North American Flyball Association at 1400 W. Devon Avenue, Box 512, Chicago, IL 60660.

Party Tricks

Teaching a dog to roll over and play dead is not as noble as training it to rescue lost children in the woods, nor does it offer the glory of the show ring or competitive canine sports; but for those people (and dogs) of limited ambition, the perfection of a few party tricks can be a ball. *Lew Burke's Dog Training* explains exactly how to teach your puppy these especially impressive feats:

- *The Zig-Zag.* As you walk forward, the dog passes between your legs at every step. "For this trick," Mr. Burke advises, "you need a dog [whose] height does not exceed the bottom of your groin."
- *Addition.* A dog is taught to appear to solve any mathematical problem with an answer less than ten. "There is no form of training more exact, punctual, and binding," Mr. Burke says.
- *Answering the Telephone.* (This is truly useful skill many service dogs perform for the hearing impaired)
- *Walking on Hind Legs.* "Boxy dogs are best. Also the dog should be at least eight months old so that his back legs are fairly well developed."
- *Dancing.* This trick should be attempted only with those dogs who have mastered walking on their hind legs.
- *Play Dead.* Instruction for this time-honored trick begins thus: "Say 'BOOM' and exactly at that moment poke a dowel, not too hard, against the dog's left shoulder and simultaneously snap the lead down. . . ."

CLEMENSTEIN

The fact that Clementine was a monster was no longer a family secret. Her behavior was so frightful that we began to call her Clemenstein, and Jane scribbled doodles on the notepad next to the phone that showed a brindle Bullmastiff with bolts emerging from her squared-off forehead.

It wasn't only we whose lives were being ravaged. Bunny and Jean, who alternate staying at our house when we travel for business, began to hint at combat pay. Jean, an unflappable veterinary technician and fearless horsewoman, left us frantic notes about Clementine's aberrant antics, kindly suggesting several dog obedience books, classes, and instructional videos we might want to look into. Bunny, also an old hand around dogs and an avid reader of self-help books, offered her own diagnosis. "Clementine has obsessive-compulsive disorder," she said. "She knows she isn't supposed to do something bad, she knows the consequences, but she has to do it anyway. She is insane."

We finally decided to tell Mimi our woes. Like the concerned breeder she is, she came to visit the next day and observe. She sat in the den where she watched Clementine pace and pant. "She is very busy," Mimi said with characteristic understatement. "Doesn't she ever stop?"

To Mimi's breeder eye, the aggravating behavior was no worse than the white stripe down the middle of Clemmy's face. Mimi didn't come right out and say she was a truly awful creature, but we saw the look of horror in her eyes when we reminded her that our book *Dog Eat Dog* was due to be published in a few weeks and that media people would be coming to our house to interview us. They would no doubt want to know all about Clementine's lineage and they would probably want to take a picture of her to run with their story. "I will bring Sam over for every interview," said Mimi. "Or you can bring reporters to my house." It was a gracious gesture, but we could read the subtext. It reminded us of the gothic novel convention of locking the weird relative away in the attic when company came.

Mimi left with no immediate solutions for us, although she did acknowledge that Clementine was more "athletic" then any Bullmastiff she had ever seen. We agreed with this observation. She leaped effortlessly over furniture, doing tumblesaults through the living room; outdoors, she ran down squirrels and crows, speeding wildly to all corners of the yard so fueled with raging puppy juice that she looked like she should have a cartoonist's blast of wind drawn at her tail and blurred circles as legs.

Jane began taking long, solitary drives to buy things she didn't need at stores she didn't want to go to. She had to get away from the puppy from hell, and any destination would do. She cried in the car, frustrated over Clementine's behavior and her inability to do anything about it. Hours later she returned home with red-rimmed eyes and a backseat full of plastic storage containers, or two dozen washcloths from Kmart. With her return, Michael would bolt. Exhausted from his shift with Clementine, he spent hours working out at the gym or target-shooting at the gun range, fantasizing about how much firepower would be necessary to stop an adrenaline-pumped puppy.

If Clementine was purely awful, we might have been able to deal with the situation better. If she was vicious we would have put her down. Like all good breeders Mimi would have taken her back if we had asked her to, and she would have tried to place her with another family or keep her herself. We could have wiped our hands of the whole harrowing situation. But the problem was that on those rare occasions when Clementine did behave herself, or when she was napping, she was positively adorable. One night, Michael suggested that since we only liked her when she was asleep, perhaps we ought to have her stuffed and mounted.

Now approaching a year old, she had grown into a big chunky mega-puppy. Her brindle coat gleamed in variegated autumn hues of brown and gold and red. Although she was no beauty by official Bullmastiff standards, she was gradually morphing into something unique and rather appealing in an offbeat way. Her eyes were bright with joy, and even when she was most exasperating, we couldn't help but admire the unbridled life force that drove her on. For all her crimes and misdemeanors she was an extremely loving dog. She could not get close enough to either of us. She was not content merely to sit near us; she wanted to be *on* us, or more accurately, *in* us. She pushed against us with her head as if she was trying to drill her way through. She ceaselessly tried to climb into our laps, lick our legs, press her head close to any part of us she could get close to, jump in the bathtub with us, and sneak into bed.

There were also our own stubborn sides to be reckoned with. We are not ones to let go of a difficult situation easily. We had not ridden out the waves of a twenty-six-year marriage and the ego clashes of working together by running away from our problems. We prided ourselves on our tenacity, and we were determined that a misbehaving puppy would not be the hill we would die on.

Despite all the problems, we had bonded with her. We could no more get rid of her than a parent can discard a misbehaving child.

Parnell Makes
the Grade

Like a fine old Ivy League college, the Guiding Eyes campus in Yorktown Heights, New York, is a quiet, pleasant place—a series of low-slung buildings on a grassy, tree-shaded lawn with a small dormitory building, veterinary facility, and gracious home now serving as offices. Despite its pacific appearance, the atmosphere is palpably different from a university, more like a convent or religious order. It is a place fraught with mission and purpose. From CEO William Badger to the volunteer kennel assistants, everyone is tuned to the same emotional channel: *We are here to change lives.*

When puppy raisers bring their dogs back for final evaluation by the Guiding Eyes staff, an event known as the In-For-Training Test, the air is positively electric. About a half dozen puppy raisers line up in a row, each with their dog, and they are run through a gamut of tests similar to those used on seven-week-old puppies.

Despite the efforts of the puppy trainers and notwithstanding the excellent gene pools from which these puppies came, about one out of three young dogs doesn't make it through the tests. Standards are high because the time and talent of the trainers who will work with them are precious; only those with a very good possibility of success are allowed to continue.

In-For-Training marks a formal end to the puppy's relationship with the people who have raised it. Puppy raisers await the outcome of this big day with a mixture of hope and sadness. Pride in the creature they have reared makes them root for the now-mature dog to succeed; and as good people for whom doing service is a way of life, they want their dog to go out into the world and become an honorable servant of the blind. On the other hand, success means they must give the animal up to the school, and to a new master. They may never see it again. If the young dog with which they have bonded so closely during the last eighteen months fails the test, puppy raisers are usually given the option to keep it as a pet.

Russ Post, the senior vice president of Guiding Eyes for the Blind, is the man in charge. Mr. Post is tall and athletic, with the square jaw and big voice of a stage actor. His is a presence to make any dog pay attention, but today he comes equipped with more than his natural way with animals. He carries a clear plastic bag that holds a .32 caliber pistol and a box of blank shells, plus a closed red-and-white striped beach umbrella.

"These puppies are in a new place, with new handlers, so they are stressed already," he tells us. "What we do today is pile on a little more stress to their current situation in order to see what they are going to do. Will they cut and run or will they get over it?"

One by one, Russ asks each handler to have his or her puppy sit, stay, and come on command. Despite being with experienced puppy-raising families for more than a year, some seem to have learned nothing . . . or perhaps they are so distracted by the new surroundings, they have forgotten everything they know. There is a considerable amount of dog-to-dog barking and wiggling with glee. Some dogs grow visibly bored at the sit, and start getting antsy; others are so sanguine they appear to be nodding off.

Parnell has learned enough not to openly carouse with others, but having been raised his whole life with Matthew and having made many other dog friends in his travels, he simply cannot resist the temptation of sidling up to his fellow enlistees in an attempt to instigate a tousle. While on a "down" command, he executes a well-practiced frog-crawl, which involves lying flat on his stomach and pretending to be still, but inching toward potential playmates like a soldier sneaking along the ground, the assumption being that if he slithers on the floor very slowly, no one will notice that he is getting close to the dogs he wants to harass. When he tried this at home or at meetings of the puppy-raising club, Dan and Susan always caught him, and always managed to keep him from getting far, but Parnell inadvertently learned how pleasant it is to lie with all fours stretched out and the earth—or linoleum—pressed cool and smooth against his belly. It had become a signature posture for him, even at home, lying like a black-furred Superman in flight.

Handlers are asked to walk the dogs one by one down a long paved corridor that runs in front of the dormitory building. "Cover 'em up!" Russ calls out—a warning for onlookers to cover their ears—then he fires the pistol into the air. This is a test to see how a puppy's nerves respond to the kind of sudden noises every guide dog might encounter at some time in life—if not a gunshot, a fourth of July fireworks display, a truck's backfire, or merely a slamming door. Amazingly, not one dog appears panicked by the sudden, loud report. Russ now asks each handler to lead the dog at a walk toward him. As the dog approaches, Russ suddenly pulls the closed striped umbrella from behind his back and snaps it open right in the animal's face. This time, every dog is startled; but some are so terrified they cower and pull hard on the leash to try to run away. Russ reaches out to pet the frightened ones, to see if a kind gesture will help them recover. Each dog reacts differently. Some step back, assess the situation, then cautiously sniff the big red-and-white nylon monster. Others will not be calmed and struggle at the end of their leash, trying to flee. Each handler then leads the dog past Russ, who suddenly rattles the umbrella to note their reaction to a dangerous sound from behind.

The umbrella test is repeated three times. A few dogs get more scared each time; one trembly yellow lab refuses even to approach Russ on the third pass. Another dog barks and growls ferociously as the handler leads it toward the scary thing. Other dogs—including Parnell—begin to suspect the umbrella won't bite them and are less frightened the second time. On the third pass, their tails are wagging; the umbrella has become fun.

While it winds up looking like some sort of game or exercise, the gunshot and the umbrella test are serious business. Imagine you are blind and walking along a city street with your dog in harness. A car backfires, someone flaps their overcoat, a bag of groceries suddenly spills in our path. If your dog tucks his tail between his legs and runs for cover, you are as vulnerable as a bird without wings. Or suppose your dog starts a fight with a dog or cat who happens past, or gets distracted from his duties by a comely bitch. Unacceptable. A guide dog must be absolutely unflappable and undistractable, smart enough to know real danger from merely scary things, and able to lead its master through any obstacles in the way.

Parnell makes the cut. In August, 1996, Dan and Susan Fisher-Owens say a teary good-bye and drive home with an empty place on their backseat. Their pup will now become the ward of trainers Sue McCahill and Jessica Sanchez, whose job it is to spend four hard months training him in all the skills he needs to be a guide dog, then to teach a blind person to use him.

For Parnell, the transformation from the Fisher-Owens home to his new life as a trainee is dramatic. Along with a class of seventeen other dogs just under two years old, he takes up residence in the kennels on the Guiding Eyes campus. This transition from home to kennel, which could be devastating for a dog of nervous temperament, is yet another test of the guide dogs' poise; and furthermore, in a paradoxical way it sets them up perfectly for the time they are transferred to their blind master. Having known the bliss of home life for nearly two years with a puppy-raising family, they understand full well how pleasant it is to be a house dog. Four months in a cacophonous kennel while undergoing rigorous daily training is like a stint in the army for a young man. It may be exciting, even fun; but when you get out, you appreciate the comforts of home all the more.

Two instructors train each class of dogs. To become an instructor requires a three-year apprenticeship, and demands such qualities as patience, devotion, an unflagging love of dogs, and an awesome dedication to making other people's lives better. Parnell's group is overseen by Sue McCahill and Jessica Sanchez, who spend every day training the eighteen dogs for a class of twelve blind people. (The six extras are "backups," in case a dog-human match doesn't work out.) The four months is basic training: sidewalk and curb work, clearances at doorways and obstacles, escalators, elevators, train platforms, crowded subways, sidewalk grates, every traffic situation imaginable, and places where there is no traffic and not even a sidewalk. As the dogs progress, the trainers increase the pressure, piling on stress: unforeseen obstacles, swerving cars, loud noises. They force the dog to make decisions in troublesome situations and to learn to take any and all hazards in stride. In four months, they transform their callow young recruits into dogs that are leaders of men and women.

CLEMENTINE:
WHEN BAD PUPPIES
HAPPEN TO GOOD PEOPLE

Perhaps we had been watching too many talk shows and listening to too many radio psychologists, but the more we thought about our problems with Clementine, the more we considered the term *hyperactivity.* Attention Deficit Disorder was the trendy diagnosis of the day; and it seemed that every child who would once have been labeled a brat was now considered a victim of ADD. The cause: a chemical imbalance; the solution: the drug Ritalin. Legions of experts were attesting to the fact that youngsters who once had to be peeled off the wall were now, thanks to Ritalin, focused and thoughtful.

We looked at Clementine pacing and panting, her eyes as large as teacups. She had been checked many times by our regular vet, who said she was the picture of health. "Maybe she really has some wires crossed," Jane suggested. "Maybe she has ADD."

"Maybe," Michael said with an I'll-try-anything shrug. And the next day we placed a call to a board-certified canine neurologist in New York State.

With us at the end of our rope and Clementine at the end of her leash, we arrived at the doctor's office for a consultation. His walls were hung with degrees from top veterinary schools around the country. Here was an expert who was clearly the Big Kahuna of dog brains. He would fix what was wrong.

Jane began the consultation by exclaiming, "I am ready to kill this dog if she doesn't behave."

There was a long pause, which the doctor broke by saying, "Before euthanasia, I would like to do a workup on her."

We flinched. He had taken Jane literally. He really thought we wanted Clementine put to sleep. Jane often speaks with dramatic hyperbole, which the doctor had no way of knowing, but we were shocked by his assumption. Of course there had been hundreds of times in the last few months when out of frustration we had wished Clementine dead, but never for a minute did we mean it literally. We were not puppy killers, a point we tried to make abundantly clear before the doctor took her into his examination room to perform some tests away from us. We were still pledging our love for her as he led her away.

We waited a long time. We read and reread all his diplomas and perused the medical textbooks that we prayed might contain an answer to our plight. Finally the doctor reappeared with Clementine, who was wagging her tail as brightly as when she had left. He handed us back the leash.

"I think she is a very healthy dog," he said. "She has no apparent neurological problems. I think you should hire a vet I know who trained at Cornell and now does behavioral consultations in the home. Call her and see what she thinks. If she strikes out, we could consider medication, but for now, no chemical treatment is called for."

We paid the four-hundred-dollar bill at the front desk and left, disheartened. Jane couldn't stop thinking that the neurologist had written "Owner wants dog dead" on his records. She fretted that he would call our regular veterinarian or our town's dog warden to warn them about us and to ask one of them to make an emergency intervention on behalf of the endangered puppy.

Worse, the doctor had no magic bullet to offer. Clementine's problem was not a simple chemical imbalance that a prescription could cure. No, it seemed that we were just another hapless couple with a badly behaved puppy. In all our smug years of perfect pet ownership, we had always looked down our noses at people with yipping, bothersome dogs, dogs that chewed furniture, dogs that wouldn't sit still, dogs that defied their masters. When such people moaned that it was the dog's fault, not theirs, we knew better. But now we had joined the losers' club ourselves.

Upon returning from the neurologist, Clementine took a dump in the kitchen and ate most of it before we discovered it and chased her away. What she didn't eat she stepped in and tracked all along the

Oriental rug in the hall. As we cleaned up she ran into the den and bared her teeth at Lewis. Then, bored with that, she ripped a hole in her dog bed and pulled out all the stuffing. Once in her crate, she barked most of the night.

All the knowledge, advice, and experience we had tried to apply to this canine demon had failed. We had no idea where to turn. We drank scotch, put in earplugs, and fell into a deep dreamless sleep.

Training Dogma

"My method is based on the fact that a dog is a dog. He is not an intelligent pupil with human logic, but rather an animal who lives in a world without human logic. To the dog, black is black and white is white. Learning is not accomplished through logical thinking, but solely through the faculty of memory presented through the medium of dog psychology, never *human* psychology."
—Lew Burke, *Lew Burke's Dog Training,* 1976

"In training, you teach the dog to reassure herself by increasing her sense of control over her handler and the world."
—Vicki Hearne, *Bandit,* 1991

"Dogs like training if the owners make it exciting enough. The best owners are outgoing, full of fun, yet gentle and loving as well as firm, and if necessary can appear angry if the dog transgresses."
—Barbara Woodhouse, *No Bad Dogs,* 1978

"I do not subscribe to fashionable arguments that dogs are slaves—although legally, of course, people do own their animals and with the bounds of defined cruelty possess the power of life and death over them—nor do I believe them to be surrogate children or toys for my amusement. These descriptions are categorically incorrect, poor metaphors that at best reflect the attitudes and behavior of certain people towards their animals. Dogs cannot be slaves or children or royalty. They can only be dogs. The people who are most successful in training, handling, even breeding dogs today—and I suspect throughout time—are those who recognize that reality."
—Mark Derr, *Dog's Best Friend,* 1997

"The outcome of undue emphasis on discipline and obedience is the production of a fawning, characterless dog of an unattractively submissive kind. The secret where dogs are concerned is to aim at a happy medium—to balance ultimate control with as much freedom as possible."

—Desmond Morris, *Dog Watching*, 1986

"Whatever your circumstances, disposition, or inclinations, you have sufficient time and ability to teach [your dog] four simple things; and for your own reputation, and that of your dog, and for the good name of dogs in general, I beg you to do it. These four fundamentals are: to obey your whistle or call; to be cleanly in your own house or the houses of your friends; not to welcome visitors by jumping all over them; and to behave in such a way in your car that you can invite a friend for a ride without subjecting your passenger to constant mauling and general discomfort. You are fairly successful in obeying ten commandments in regard to your own conduct; you should be able to obey only four for regulating the conduct of your dog."

—William Cary Duncan, *Dog Training Made Easy*, 1940

"Obedience is the basis of all training. At first, the dog, like humans, does what he thinks he can get away with. In many cases, the certainty of punishment keeps him from such acts as soiling, chewing a curtain, sneaking food from the kitchen table; and yet, most acts of the dog are done willingly, with pleasure and out of the great overpowering desire which every dog has— to win the approval, the pat of the hand, and the kindly spoken word of the master."

—Will Judy, *Care of the Dog*, 1948

"A dog loves the challenge that you toss to his alertness. Your dog has understanding—intuition—and a wisdom far beyond your human ken.

"You need not lift your voice. You need not raise your hand to him to make him understand or follow your instructions. You need only to be yourself, the master whom he loves and respects with dog-like devotion.

"Remember your eyes are his looking glass. Your thoughts are louder to him than the beat of a drum. And though words may be a language, your silence is your eloquence when you speak to your dog."

—Beth Brown, *Everybody's Dog Book*, 1953

"In every kind of training which demands active cooperation on the part of the dog, as in jumping, retrieving, and other feats, we must not forget that even the best dog possesses no human sense of duty and, in sharp contrast to quite small children, will only collaborate as long as he is enjoying the work. . . . At all costs we must make the animal feel that he is not obliged but permitted to carry out the exercise in question."

—Conrad Lorenz, *Man Meets Dog*, 1954

"We are to listen to a dog until we discover what is needed instead of imposing ourselves in the name of training. . . . Discipline methods that reflect instinctual canine behavior will communicate displeasure in ways a dog can understand. Other corrections like throwing or hitting the dog with objects, spanking with newspapers, or simple pleading only serve human, not canine ends."

—The Monks of New Skete, *How to Be Your Dog's Best Friend*, 1978

"One handler mistake is trying to get the upper hand with the dog. The dog needs a sense of self-confidence, and it acquires this when the trainer shows it respect, so both dog and handler trust each other. There must be a true human-dog partnership."

—Dr. Janet Ruckert, *Are You My Dog?*, 1989

"Like any close relationship between two people, there will be an occasional clash of interests if not of wills, and you must work this out without loss of intimacy."

—George Bird Evans, *Troubles with Bird Dogs*, 1975

"Dogs are very similar to persons inasmuch as each has his own personality. . . . Therefore by careful assignment of men and dogs these traits were put to the best advantage. For example—a handler who was deliberate and methodical in his actions would be assigned a dog possessed with the tendency of over anxiety and possible nervousness. In training, the handler's deliberateness and patience would help subdue the anxiety of the dog. . . . By the same method, animals which were slow in actions were assigned to handlers who were quick in movements."

—John Behan, *Dogs of War*, 1946

"A fearful puppy may have no idea where her body stops and the rest of the world begins. Give that dog a sense of her body; and from that, self-confidence flows. It is also important to give her a name that sounds right. If her name sounds like a bark or a growl, that is what you'll get. Sound is so important to a puppy; that is why I 'tone' more than I speak when I work with any animal: it goes right to their brain waves."

—Linda Tellington-Jones, author of *The Tellington Ttouch*,
at a Phoenix, Arizona, dog-training seminar, February 1993

"No one should think, regardless of what species the dog is, that it can be trained only by being beaten; on the contrary, every trainer should make it his duty, when his animal has done well in his exercises, to pet him and make him a faithful friend, now and then giving him some delicacy to eat. It is only in this way that the dog will show his willingness and obedience to his master and will become attached and faithful until death."

—Jacob Birrer, *The Story of His Life*, Germany, 1845

WILL JUDY'S SEVENTEEN TRAINING DON'TS

1. Don't punish your dog while you are angry or lack control of yourself.

2. Don't punish your dog with the leash or any instrument of training he should associate with duty or pleasure.

3. Don't sneak up on your dog or grab him from the rear.

4. Don't chase your dog to catch him; he must come to you or run after you.

5. Don't coax your dog to you and then turn upon him with the whip. You will regret the deception.

6. Don't trick or fool or taunt your dog. It is a cruel and inconsistent act to tease your dog to come to you when he cannot.

7. Don't punish a dog by stepping on his paws needlessly. They are extremely sensitive. Don't twist his ears playfully or otherwise. Never strike him on the backbone, on the loin, or in the face.

8. Don't grab your dog or reach for him quickly. He should never fear his master, should not be made nervous by his master, and should feel that punishment given him is deserved.

9. Don't nag your dog; don't be giving orders to him constantly; don't pester him with your shoutings.

10. Don't praise a dog for doing a certain act, then at a later time, scold him for doing the same act. If you permit him to bite your toes and think it fun today, do not strike him for doing it tomorrow, when you are not in a good humor. Consistency is a chief virtue in dog training.

11. Don't train your dog immediately or soon after he has eaten.

12. Don't lose patience with a puppy younger than six months. Never throw a puppy or kick a puppy nor lift him by the head or leg or skin of the neck.

13. Don't train him in feats requiring much strength or endurance until he is at least six months old.

14. Don't work your dog without some short rest or play periods during the period of training. A five-minute rest for every fifteen minutes of training is desirable.

15. Don't permit everyone to give commands to your dog. While you are training him, he must be a one-man dog, depending on you alone to feed him and care for him.

16. Don't consider tricks the chief end or the chief part of training of the dog. Usefulness is the object sought in all instruc-

tion of the dog. Acts that spring naturally from the dog's instincts are the acts to be fostered.

17. Don't expect your dog to be a wonderful dog after a few weeks of training; four months to a year may be necessary in order to make his master proud of him, but the work is worth the effort. Training never ends.

—Will Judy, *Training the Dog*, 1932

Parnell:

Guiding Eyes

The most precious thing a guide dog can give to a blind person is the sort of basic independence sighted people take for granted. Before Morris Frank and his German Shephered Buddy led the way, starting in 1929 (see appendix, p. 180), to be blind was to be profoundly helpless. The generally accepted image of a blind person back then was of a pitiful beggar, dependent on others simply to cross the street. Much progress has been made, and passage of the Americans with Disabilities Act was supposed to ensure equal opportunity, but to this day, only a small fraction of blind people are able to support themselves.

The impotence of being blind is a notion that persists, even—perhaps *especially*—among many who are afflicted. "I went for years without a dog because I was humiliated," explains Stephen Kuusisto, director of alumni relations at Guiding Eyes, and blind since birth. "I walked around as though I could see, denying my blindness. I navigated with a white cane . . . and there were so many close calls." Steve is in his late thirties, dressed in a leather bomber jacket, *GQ*-level shirt and tie, with a set of wire-rimmed shades that veil his unseeing eyes. He has taught English in college and is a published poet and autobiographer who has appeared in *Glamour* magazine and has told his story in *Planet of the Blind*. As he speaks, a four-year-old yellow lab named Corky sits patiently by his side at the desk in his office. When he stands to greet someone who walks in the door, Corky stands, too. As long as Steve keeps the harness on her, she remains with him—she is all business, waiting for a cue. But unhooking the harness is a signal to Corky that she can rest at ease. She toddles over to sniff strangers, then rolls on her back inviting someone to pet her soft belly.

Steve recalls that shortly after he finally decided to get a dog five years ago, he thought *why in the hell did it take me this long? I love dogs!* "I came into this school a two-legged human," he says. "I am now a creature with six legs." Steve appears to stroke and play with Corky the way anyone would treat a pet dog they like; but beyond that familiar human-pet affection is a bond that ordinary pet owners never can know. "What a feeling it is to have transmitted up the harness handle a sense of alertness, a certain knowledge that the dog is watching out," Steve says. "It is magic, it is liberating, it is indescribable to feel that after so many years of uncertainty. A guide dog is not just your eyes. A guide dog is your freedom."

The meaning of a guide dog to a blind person—and of master to dog—is expressed vividly in Morris Frank's *First Lady of the Seeing Eye,* toward the end of which Frank tells about his final walk with America's first Seeing Eye dog, Buddy:

> On the last morning she led me from the apartment to the car. I had to help hold her up with the harness, because she was too weak to stand alone. At the office she would not stay in her place but kept coming over to me. She wanted to be near me all the time, so I took her back and sat on the edge of her bed and stroked her lovely head.
>
> There in the sunshine that streamed in through a window, the gallant creature shivered with cold. We put a blanket around her and I patted her. At last, she reached up, gave my tear-stained face a loving lick, and then dropped to well-earned sleep. . . .
>
> We laid her to her last rest, wearing her harness and leash. . . . As I told her, "You're a good girl," for the last time, I realized that my debt to Buddy is greater than I can ever tell. She gave me courage to do things that I would never have attempted had she not come into my life.

Why Labs?

The first two canine graduates of the Guiding Eyes for the Blind breeding program, in 1956, were Boxers that had been donated to the school. For many years thereafter, Guiding Eyes dogs were acquired the way the earliest Seeing Eye dogs came into service in America in the 1930s: either as donations or from shelters. Program graduates were a varied lot of several kinds of pure-breds as well as mixed-breeds that met these criteria:

- easy coat care
- big enough to do the job (generally 50–80 pounds)
- good health
- steady temperament

Many fine guide dogs thus acquired went into the world to live lives of service, but it became apparent over time that relying on rescued dogs from the shelter and donations from breeders wasn't good enough. Although even a badly-behaved dog can be retrained for guide work, it sometimes happened that the inappropriate behavior—suppressed but not entirely eliminated by the G.E.B. trainers—would reoccur months later once the dog went into service; furthermore, unforeseen health problems could rear up at any time. "We needed predictability," breeding center director Jane Russenberger says. "When you breed your own dogs, you can focus your resources. Less time is wasted on ones that don't work out."

In the 1960s, a breeding colony was begun, and today nearly all guide dogs that are given to graduates of the program come from that colony. There are still a few exceptional leaders that come into the program as donations when they are young puppies. But an extremely well-planned and meticulously documented eugenics program is the source of most.

In the beginning, the colony had a majority of Golden Retrievers; and goldens are still very much part of the program; but gradually labs came to dominate the breeding stock because of their solid, working temperaments and good health. There are some German Shepherd studs and brood bitches, too, but even fewer than there are goldens. Boxers have been phased out and are not part of the breeding program. "Their coats are too thin to thrive in cold northern climates," Ms. Russenberger explains. "And their short muzzles can make it hard for them to breathe in severe heat. Labs can work in any climate, they are strong and athletic, and they carry a temperament that is just the right mixture of devotion and independence. We find that many German Shepherds too high-energy for guide work become service dogs of other kinds, in police work, for instance; and the goldens without that strong streak of independence that we need often go into therapy work."

Guiding Eyes head trainer Kathy Zubrycki points out that labs are so well-suited for the job because guide work usually has a pace that is similar to the retrieving work they were originally developed to do. "They need to stay with a handler in a duck blind for hours. Then when the bird drops, they go to work and do a precise, delicate job that requires stamina. After that they return to the duck blind and may have to remain calm and quiet for hours." Kathy also says that most labs have a lower body sensitivity than other breeds. "If they get stepped on in a subway or on the sidewalk, they don't seem to mind as much. They can adapt to the stress of a noisy city or the stress of a lonely farmhouse with relative ease. Plus they have coats that don't require a half-hour's grooming each morning."

America's reliance on labs for guide work is not reflected in other countries' preferences; there is a school in New Zealand that trains Dalmatians; successful programs elsewhere breed Border Collies, Australian Shepherds, golden/lab crosses, and even Bouviers de Flandres for guide work.

"I'm not saying that I don't keep my eye open for other breeds' potential," Jane Russenberger says, "but for the next twenty years at least, labs will rule. To develop a breeding colony like we have takes so much time and money; and at first, so many dogs are culled out; but as the gene pool is improved, more and more dogs are suitable for guide work. One reason we have been successful is that we share resources with other programs around the world that are producing excellent guide dogs. You cannot constantly return to the same gene pool. Going out is a way of always improving and keeping it healthy. Our goal is to produce the finest labs the world has ever seen."

PARNELL'S PARTNER

Cindy Blair, blinded by illness at the age of eighteen, knows the difference a guide dog can make and the freedom it allows. Now a wife, a mother of a teenage son, a caterer, and president of the PTA at her son's Jesuit school in the suburbs of Rochester, New York, Cindy was suddenly rendered dependent all over again in September 1996, after her second guide dog, Brent, underwent a routine cystectomy. The surgery left a scar just where the harness pressed against his skin, and even after he healed, the ordinary cues of pulling and tugging on the harness caused him enough pain to make him veer off course. The harness is a crucial means of communication between dog and human; Brent's aversion to it meant the end of his service career. So although he was willing and ready to get back to work—as he had been trained to do from puppyhood—Brent went into forced early retirement. He become the Blair family pet, just as Cindy's first guide dog, Andrew, had been retired when he became too infirm to work ten years earlier.

"I am a bird with a broken wing," Cindy announces when she arrives at the Guiding Eyes campus in Yorktown Heights on January 7, 1997. Cindy is indeed reminiscent of a bird: small and fragile, quick, intense, and vigilant. When she moves, even without a dog, there is a strong sense of purpose to her; she is a take-charge woman, apparently unfazed by blindness. She wears no dark glasses, and until you speak closely with her and notice that her sharp, deep brown eyes don't focus on yours, you might never know she cannot see.

Cindy is one of a class of twelve blind people who have come to Guiding Eyes to be paired with a dog during a concentrated three-week session. Although the cost of training a guide dog is $25,000, none of the students are required to pay anything. The cost of raising and training each dog, as well as of lifetime support of the dog even beyond its useful term in service, are borne by Guiding Eyes, whose budget comes entirely from voluntary contributions.

Cindy calls herself a "retread," meaning she had a guide dog before and is already familiar with the feel of the harness in her hand, as are five of her classmates. Six of the group, who range in age from eighteen to fifty, have never had a guide dog. Some have been blind all their lives; others recently lost their sight due to illness or accident. Although students come to Guiding Eyes from throughout the world—Israel in particular sends many blinded war veterans—all the members of this January class are Americans. Training sessions for blind people run throughout the year, with just a few days between graduation and the arrival of new students; most of this January class have come from cold northern parts of the country. They are people untroubled by the prospect of working outdoors with their new canine partners during a northeast winter.

When they arrive on campus Tuesday, the twelve students are assigned rooms in the dorm—mostly doubles. Each room is clean, tidy, and functional, with a radio but no TV and no art on the cinder-block walls. There are two doors, one that opens into an interior hall, another that leads directly to the lawn outside, making it easy for students to learn to "park" their dogs—the school's preferred euphemism for taking them out to defecate. "Spell it backward!" instructors tell students who don't immediately understand.

Emotions in the dorm rooms and at the tables in the communal dining room are intense. Retreads like Cindy are thrilled with anticipation, eager to meet their new dogs. Other students, such as Bob Serrano of Albany, are deeply anxious. Bob has never had a guide dog; he has never had any kind of pet animal, and frankly, he feels uncomfortable around them. He yearns for the freedom that a dog could bring him, but he really doesn't know if he has what it takes. Bob is a strapping man with a bushy crew cut and a sports jogging suit. He is newly blind, and the notion of having to depend on an animal to reenter the world fills him with panic.

With Kathy Zubrycki, the school training supervisor, the team of two instructors have scrutinized the dogs and have considered what they know about the students and have made their best guess as to which dog will fit which student. It is a big decision to pair a person with a dog that will be its guiding eyes for perhaps ten years. The important thing is to match the personality and physical talents of the dog to the demands of the owner. "It is mostly about footwork and pace," Kathy says to explain how the decision is made. "Do they travel by bus? Do they live in an area with sidewalks? How fast do they move? How often do they go out?" Aesthetics also play a part in the pairing: Will the dog be a good physical match for its master? Rarely would a tiny, frail person be matched with a boisterous 110-pound German Shepherd; and a dainty yellow lab wouldn't likely be given to a big man who pumps iron for a hobby. To some degree, the matches are made based on the intangible instincts of the trainers, who have seen so many dogs and masters paired up.

To confirm their hunches about the mating of specific dogs to particular people, and to help the novice students gain some sense of what it is like to use a dog as their guide, instructors spend the first two days of the session taking each blind person on what is called the Juno walk (after the Roman goddess known as a protector of women). After breakfast, the students bundle up in their thermal coats, gloves, hats, and mufflers and two Guiding Eyes vans carry them into the village of Yorktown Heights. They park on a block in front of a strip mall where there is some traffic and where there are two nearby intersections, but not many pedestrians. It is a bitterly cold day; plumes of exhaust smoke puff from the tailpipes as the vans idle and one by one, each student steps out for the walk.

For the Juno walk, each student is given the end of a harness to hold, and the trainer acts like a dog. They don't actually get down on all fours; they hold the end where the dog would be harnessed and lead the blind person around the way a dog would do it . . . but in this instance, a dog that can speak and tell the person at the other end of the harness what to do and what not to do. The trainers know exactly how the dogs will deal with everything encountered on the street—they have worked painstakingly with them for four months, bringing them to a point of 100 percent reliability, so long as they get the right cues.

It is strange to see the human trainers in harness like a dog with the blind person following behind. In some cases it shocks unaware pedestrians. Trainer Sue McCahill, an athletic, honey-haired blonde, leads Henry Tucker, a blind African-American man, through the paces. As Sue shows Henry how to navigate around a bus stop enclosure, she purposely lets him walk smack into the side of one to let him learn from his mistake while she is in the harness. An older black lady in a turban, waiting for the bus, gasps. "Why you leading that black boy into a wall!? Can't you see, he's blind!" The woman curses as Sue drags Henry around the wall and down the street. Sue is too busy to take anything personally, or even to laugh at how weird an image the Juno walk presents to the outside world.

Lunch on the second day of the program in the Guiding Eyes dining room is especially boisterous, like a high school cafeteria the first week of the semester. The twelve students are thrilled about meeting their dogs at one o'clock that afternoon. Craig Hedgecock, a social worker and a musician, taps out a tune on the table with his spoon and knife. Some residents table-hop to talk to new friends and compare wish lists about the dog they know will soon be theirs.

The class of twelve blind people gather in the Campbell Lounge near the dining area, finding chairs along one wall, so head trainer Kathy Zubrycki can brief them. Kathy, a handsome woman who looks like she could have been a ranch wife in Montana a hundred years ago, sits by the fireplace flanked by Jessica Sanchez and Sue McCahill, who have worked so closely with the eighteen dogs since September and have used all their knowledge and intuition to pair them up with the right people. One member of the class, jittery with anticipation, grins as the thought dawns on him: "I guess this is the ultimate blind date."

Jessica and Sue chuckle nervously; they feel the awesome responsibility of matchmaking *twelve* blind dates. Their interest in the dates' working out well goes beyond their professionalism and their desire to help the blind people. In four months of training the dogs, they have grown tremendously attached to them; they know their strengths, weaknesses, and quirks. As they taught the dogs to respond to voice commands and harness cues, they worked through a thousand potential hazards alongside them, all in the interest of exposing them to everything life might eventually throw their way. They went to crowded shopping malls where they were taught how to lead a blind person on and off an escalator, they crossed busy city streets at rush hour, they navigated over active train tracks and along narrow footpath bridges in the woods. Some of the dogs attended the ticker-tape parade for the Yankees after the World Series. Sue and Jessica are fully confident the dogs can do a good job. And they are as weepy as a pair of proud mothers who are about to watch their handsome, well-behaved young boys join the army.

"We call this phase the turnover," Kathy tells the assembled students. "These dogs have gone from their puppy homes to a kennel, from a family to a pack. Each of those transitions was traumatic in its own way. After the kennel, the instructors came into the picture, and after four months with them, the dogs have learned exactly what to expect and who will greet them every morning. Now, the dogs are being uprooted again, and we are introducing them to you. They will be confused. But the turnover works because these dogs want to please. They want to attach themselves to somebody. That somebody is going to be you. The instructors' job now is to pull away. It will take some time. But your job is an easy one. All you have to do is love them." There is a long, silent pause as Kathy lets this thought sink in.

Kathy explains that when the students are introduced to their dogs, everything should be low-key. "Don't try any commands at all. No rough-housing, no discipline. For the first couple of days, *we* will be the bad guys. We will do all the corrections. All you have to do is bond."

As she speaks, several of the dogs play outside on the lawn, chasing each other and running after balls tossed by assistant trainers. But the glass on the sliding doors is thick enough so the students cannot hear anything; nor, of course, can they see. Their dogs are still a mystery to them. And the dogs themselves have no reason to expect that they are about to meet their partners and embark on a whole new life.

Before the actual transfer of the dogs, some of the anxiety in the Campbell Lounge is lessened by playing a little game that lets the students know their dog's name.

Addressing Murry Dimon, a kindly retread from West Seneca, New York, Kathy says, "Your dog is a black lab, male, whose name sounds like the man who parted the red sea. . . ."

"Is it Moses?" Murry queries.

"It's Moseley!" Sue bursts out. Of all the dogs they have trained, Moseley is a special favorite with Sue and Jessica. A gift to the program rather than a product of the breeding colony, Moseley is one of those magical creatures with an expression of kindness, deep sympathy, and intelligence. *Big sweet pup* were the words used to characterize him at his seven-week evaluation test, a description that still fits, even though he has become a responsible and well-trained adult dog.

Craig Hedgecock, a massively muscular young man with top ranking among collegiate wrestlers in the east, is getting his first dog. "There is a company that delivers things called Wells *blank*," Kathy says to him. "But replace the *F* with a *V*."

"Vargo?" Craig wonders.

"Yes!" says Sue, who trained Vargo

"Vargo," Craig repeats to himself. "What a cool name!"

"Esther, on Broadway there is a show called *blank Victoria.* He is a yellow lab."

"His name is Victor!" student Esther Acha calls out with glee.

When Bob Serrano is told that his dog is a yellow lab named Eagle, he says with wonder, "I dreamt of a yellow lab!"

"Linette, do you know *Star Trek?*" Kathy asks.

Linette Stevens, back for her third dog, is a woman with a birth defect that makes her as diminutive as a small child, and with a child's voice. She says she knows the TV show quite well. Many of the quiz-show questions demand a knowledge of visible popular culture, with which these active blind people seem at least as familiar as are any sighted folk. Even those who have been blind since birth seem to have absorbed a familiarity with icons that most of us think of as primarily visual.

"The main character on *Star Trek* was named Captain *blank*."

"Oh, my God!" Linette says, laughing with surprise. "My best friend's name is Kirk! How will he know who I'm calling?" Later, Linette tells us that her buddy Kirk also is blind, but additionally suffers from a severe equilibrium problem. His dog, specially trained by Kathy's husband, Ted, is one of those that serves not only as a visual guide, but as an aid to maintaining balance.

Kathy comes to Cindy Blair. "Cindy, do you remember the show *Bonanza?*"

Cindy nods, intensely curious as to where Kathy is going with this line of questioning.

"What was the name of the actor who played the oldest brother?"

"Hoss?" someone else volunteers.

"No," Kathy says. "It was *blank* Roberts."

"Pernell?" Cindy guesses.

"Parnell!" Kathy says.

"Parnell," Cindy says. She beams with the joy of knowing. "Parnell," she repeats quietly to herself. As the game continues, Cindy mouths the word *Parnell* over and over, grinning to herself.

When the game is done and everybody knows the names of their dogs, Kathy jokes, "Those of you who don't want your dogs, stay here. The rest of you—anybody who wants to meet their dog—leave the room and we will call you back one by one." As fast as twelve blind people can hurry out of an unfamiliar room into the unknown hallways of the school, the students exit the Campbell Lounge. Several feel their way to a small recreation cubicle set aside for smokers, where they light up and puff deeply. Others mill in the hallway, waiting for their names to be called.

Each student is called back by Sue or Jessica over the school's loudspeaker system. The extreme tension of meeting one's partner is almost unbearable, not only among the students but especially among Sue, Jessica, and Kathy, who know perhaps even better than the novices just how important a guide dog can become to its master. To defuse the anxiety, their loudspeaker announcements are whimsical, silly, or overly romantic.

"Spencer, oh, Spencer, there is someone waiting for you in the Campbell Lounge," Jessica croons. "Please come meet him. Bring your leash . . . but don't bring your cane."

"Hi," says Sue over the speaker. "My name is Vargo. I am waiting for Craig in the Campbell Lounge."

Craig sits in a chair at one side of the large room while Sue holds Vargo, a male German Shepherd, on the other side of the room. Sue stands and gives Vargo his command to move forward. Jessica, standing near Craig, is the dog's target, but with subtle body language and unseen cues, the two trainers direct Vargo directly into Craig. Craig is leaning off the edge of the chair, and when abruptly he feels the dog's warm breath in front of his face, he slips off the seat to the floor. The big wrestler is weak with the emotion he feels as Vargo, wriggling with doggy joy, licks him all over his face.

"He has a soft, sensitive eye," Sue says. "He has a white cross on his chest."

Craig is on the floor intertwined with Vargo. He is laughing and crying at the same time. He manages to croak out, "I'm all broken up" as he tousles with the happy dog.

Sue guides his hands to clip a leash onto Vargo's collar and helps the two of them walk out of the room together, side by side.

"I'm a-comin', I'm a-comin'," calls Alison Dolan from the hallway when her name is announced and she is summoned in to meet her dog Colleen.

"She is blond like you," Sue tells Alison. "Her belly is almost white. She has the biggest, roundest eyes." Alison hugs her little yellow lab, tears streaming down her face. She straightens up and feels for Colleen's collar, then clips on her leash. As the two walk out together, Sue is radiant with pride. This appears to be a perfect match. She cannot help but exclaim, "You look so good together already!"

Even before Murry Dimon is called in to meet Moseley, Jessica Sanchez is fighting back tears. "This is going to get messy," she says. "Moseley is so special. He is a dog who would die for you. He makes you laugh. No matter how bad you feel, he can take care of you." When he meets Murry, Moseley fairly attacks his new master with affection, mussing his neat comb-over hairdo hair with a wet nose so the hair stands up on one side of his head like a furry tidal wave. Moseley licks Murry all over his face. Murry is at first taken aback by the overload of affection, but soon he melts off his chair to the floor and puts his arms in a big hug around Moseley's neck. He tries to say something, but words fail him. He stands, trying to straighten his clothes and using his fingers to comb his mussed hair back. Emotional by nature, Jessica is also speechless, sobbing silently as she watches her favorite dog walk out the door. "He looks good on you," Kathy calls to Murry, finally breaking the silence.

Overwhelmed by emotions, Jessica is falling apart. "Oh, this is horrible," she mutters between Kleenex-muffled sniffles, barely able to regain her composure when it comes time to call Cindy Blair into the lounge. As Cindy enters, Jessica, Sue, and Kathy all sing "Happy Birthday" to her. Cindy's shallow breath is short from anticipation. She sits on the edge of a chair, aware that her new dog, Parnell, is at the opposite side of the room.

"Call him," Sue says.

"He'll come to you," says Jessica, who his holding him by the collar.

"Parnell . . ." Cindy is so short of breath that she calls his name quietly. He hears, but Jessica is still holding him. Cindy knows she has to muster more energy. "Parnell!" she calls out. Jessica lets go of the dog and Parnell lopes across the room into Cindy's arms. She hugs him and kisses him as he licks her face. "He's small," she says, her practiced hands running up and down his body. "Is he small?" The instructors don't answer. Most physical details are kept in abeyance at first meeting, the idea being to encourage students to create an image of their dog based on touch, feel, and actual contact rather than statistics. They also don't want to encourage inevitable comparisons: *my dog is bigger than your dog.*

"Oh, thank you," Cindy says, "Thank you, thank you, thank you." Jessica helps her walk out of the room and comes back looking like she needs a transfusion. The emotions of the afternoon have drained her. The ends of her long brown hair are wet with tears. Is it this emotional with every class? The three trainers nod, too spent to speak.

At six o'clock Friday morning, after their first night with a four-legged companion sleeping by the side of the bed, Guiding Eyes students are awakened by Sue McCahill calling to them over the loudspeaker: "Good morning! It is time to park and feed your dogs."

Over breakfast that morning, twelve former strangers bubble with news about how their blind dates went the night before.

"I got a wet nose in my face at three A.M.!" Alison Dolan confesses.

"Moseley was the first one out to poop and pee," Murry Dimond boasts, although he doesn't explain how he knows this fact, and no one challenges his assertion. Students and faculty alike are relishing Murry's new pride of ownership.

"I can tell when Vargo is looking at me," Craig Hedgecock testifies.

"This Valor, he's a wild guy," says Henry Tucker of his German Shepherd, which has already developed the habit of leaning against

Henry's leg to let him know exactly where he is. Henry is a gentle, soft-spoken soul, and you can see that sitting quietly takes some effort for Valor, who has all the spunk of a young, vigorous German Shepherd eager to strut his stuff. But he also has the blood and the training instinctively to know how to adjust his personality to mesh with the more easygoing ways of his new partner. Later that day when students take their first field trip into White Plains for a test walk along a simple sidewalk course with which all the dogs are already familiar—two left turns, about face, then a return to the van—Valor and Henry proceed flawlessly. Henry, who has never had a guide dog before, is awestruck by his new ability to navigate unfamiliar territory with such ease. Valor savors his opportunity to lead the way. Finally, he is doing exactly what all his instinct and all his training tell him to do, and he is doing it splendidly. If a dog could smile with pride, that's what Valor is doing. As far as this German Shepherd is concerned, the world is his oyster.

Clementine:
Bondage and Discipline

Clementine could do nothing right, and we still had no clue how to arrest her descent into criminal behavior. After consulting the canine neurologist and getting no instant cure for the problem, we tried his suggestion of calling a veterinarian/behaviorist. In anticipation of her visit, the behaviorist sent us a lengthy questionnaire and asked us to keep a detailed diary of all pet-human interactions in our house over the course of a week.

She arrived seven days later. A small, serious woman with wire-rimmed glasses and a DVM degree from Cornell, she was in a lofty category of doggy shrink, way above the run-of-the-mill self-styled trainer. She spent the better part of an afternoon watching Clementine misbehave, then she left, telling us she would mail us her observations and then we would chat. A few days later her solution arrived. She had studied our questionnaire and her own notes taken while observing Clementine and put together an analysis of the problem and a protocol for us to follow.

Her expert diagnosis was that Clementine was a pest. Not certifiable enough for medication, but scoring at the topmost level of irritating. This, we could have told her for free.

"It seems Clementine was not informed that the typical Bullmastiff takes life in stride," the doctor's analysis began. She then went on to suggest an explicit eleven-step program that centered around the use of a contraption that looked like something a bondage fetishist would wear—a complicated leash-muzzle device that wrapped around the dog's head and snout and was intended to produce submissive behavior.

The veterinarian's plan for a day in the life of Clementine was so complete that we wondered if there would be any free minutes left for us to work, eat, or sleep. Basically, we were to spend our time tethered to her while she was trussed up in the S-M suit. Desperate for anything that would take us out of the puppy purgatory our lives had become, we tried to obey the instruction sheet.

The doctor's notes included the necessity of remodeling our house, installing special tiles on the floor in the kitchen "to encourage Clementine to develop an acceptable substrate preference" for peeing. We were to continue to wake up well before dawn, so Clementine didn't have the opportunity to soil her sleeping crate. All rugs were to be sent out for professional cleaning to get rid of the seductive odor of her pee. Clementine's regular exercise routine was to be increased. Longer walks in the morning were highly recommended.

The rug-cleaning service denuded our house of stinky carpets, we bought special tiles for the kitchen, and we trussed Clementine like a Thanksgiving turkey in her new device, except when she was taken on walks long enough to make a marine boot camp instructor cry. By the third day of the rigorous new regime, Clementine was as sick of us as we were of her. We felt sorry for her, all snagged up in the stupid-looking bondage device, with her big round eyes peering over the straps. "I hate this plan," Michael finally said.

Jane agreed, and after a week, we gave up on the overly elaborate scheme, chalking it up as just one more failed attempt to live with this disturbing dog.

Anyway, it was apparent that the bondage device didn't really work. Clementine was smart enough to figure out how to behave badly even with it on. She would gnaw on the freshly cleaned rugs through her muzzle, and she could bark like a ventriloquist without moving her lips. This puppy could have taught Hannibal Lechter a trick or two.

The neurologist's bill for consultation was $350, not including the cost of Clementine's face truss. Nor did her fee include what we spent to sanitize all the rugs in the house and install "acceptable substrate tiles" in the kitchen. We figure the tab for this episode at about $1,500, not including the two satellite dish remote controls, at $95 each, that Clementine managed to crunch to smithereens through her muzzle.

What a Puppy Costs

The initial price of a puppy, amortized over its lifetime, is minimal compared to the upkeep. A fifty-pound dog with few health problems and no special needs that lives ten years will cost its owner a minimum of $12,000.

In the beginning, you will probably lay out $50 for a rescued dog from a shelter, $500 to $1,000 to a breeder for a "pet quality" purebred, or a few thousand for a puppy with great show and/or breeding potential. For a very trendy breed or a rare breed getting trendy, the law of supply and demand dictates a higher price.

In addition to the cost of the puppy itself, every new dog owner must expect to buy a few collars (as the dog's neck grows) at $10 to $20 apiece, a leash or two (figure $25 for a good one), plenty of chew toys in hopes of saving your shoes and pillows (a nice, simple toy costs between $10 and $20), food and water dishes ($10–$20 apiece), a dog bed (up to $100, depending on the size of the dog) or several dog beds if your puppy enjoys chewing his bed, and a crate ($100 for one to fit an average-size dog; more for crates that can be used in transport).

Figure spending $500 to $1,000 per year for good-quality food.

Grooming costs are breed-specific. Many short-haired dogs require only nail clipping and occasional ear cleaning, plus periodic brushing to remove shedding hair and baths when necessary; vets also recommend toothbrushing. All these procedures can easily be done at home and cost nothing more than the price of basic tools. Long-coated and double-coated dogs, on the other hand, may require clipping, shaping, or in the case of terriers to be shown, stripping, all of which are time-consuming and require some expertise. A professional dog groomer can do the job; the price varies depending on the size of the dog and the degree of difficulty. You'll pay about $50 for a trim-and-wash on a medium-size dog with no special needs.

Will you want to fence your yard? At one point, when our puppy Clementine was driving us insane, we decided to create an enclosed area where she would be able to play outdoors and thus, we hoped, leave us alone for a while. Because she was Clementine, we knew she would chew through or burrow under any ordinary fence. So we installed a "deer-guard" fence that gives a mild electric jolt if touched. Cost: $1,500. It works great, and even Clementine, zapped just once, hasn't tried to break out since.

Do you leave home long enough to require the services of a pet-sitter? Or will you be kenneling your dog when you go out of town? We pay $15 per visit for someone to stop by and walk the dogs in the afternoon if we'll be gone all day, $50 per day for someone to stay the night and tend two dogs plus a parrot. Kennel costs generally range from $20 to $50 per night per dog.

Now, we've saved the worst for last: medical bills. Being purebred aficionados, we've spent thousands—no, tens of thousands—of dollars doing what has been necessary to keep our pets healthy. It must be said that the breeds we like are high-maintenance types; it is a lucky Bulldog or Bullmastiff owner who enjoys a long-lived pet without enduring severe and costly (and emotionally trying) medical traumas. Purchased from a responsible breeder, a sturdier strain of dog, such as a Labrador Retriever, is less likely to surprise its owner with a $4,000 bill for dermatitis treatments (as our Bullmastiff Edwina once did). And mixed breeds, with the strength of biodiversity in their genes, have an even greater chance of staying healthy at low cost.

Still, anyone who buys any dog should be prepared to deal with unforeseen medical expenses. When she was nearly two, the luckless Clementine developed chronic impacted anal sacs, causing her to scoot her ass along the rug to squeeze out the hideous-smelling fluid. Cost of her anal sacculectomy: $750, not including shampooing every rug in the house.

We once received a desperate phone call from a woman who

lived in a trailer camp in Maine who had saved her money for a few years so she could afford to buy her dream purebred puppy. As the dog grew, it developed a painful and life-threatening skin rash. She could not afford the medical treatments, and she lived hundreds of miles from the nearest canine dermatologist, anyway. Her dream puppy wound up with the breed rescue group, which was able to place it with someone who had the money and the charitable soul to care for it.

One way to deal with unexpected medical expenses is canine health insurance. Like its human counterpart, it is a complicated business. The cost can range from a few hundred to a thousand dollars a year, depending on the age of the dog, what exactly you want covered, deductibles, and lifetime limits. Two companies that offer a range of policies are Anipals (1-888-ANI-PALS) and Veterinary Pet Insurance (1-800-872-7387.) Pet Assure (1-888-789-PETS) is like an HMO in that it covers only visits to participating veterinarians, groomers, and kennels. The most expensive programs will reimburse policy holders for pre-existing conditions, hereditary ailments, and even certain elective procedures. Basic coverage only pays for some emergencies and can have a low ceiling and high copayments for medication.

Catastrophic illness aside, there are some medical costs almost any puppy buyer can count on. To spay or neuter a dog runs about $250 at a private vet; or you can call 1-800-248-SPAY to find a low-cost spay-neuter clinic near you. (This is another good reason to get one from a shelter: they provide that service for free or at a reduced rate.) Monthly heartworm pills, yearly rabies shots, parvo vaccines, flea and tick prevention or treatment will run a minimum of $100 per year. Such medical nonemergencies as minor wounds, runny eyes, deep cleaning of the ears, expulsion of the anal sacs, and hot spots on the coat are all best dealt with by a veterinary pro; in our neighborhood, an office visit runs $40 plus the cost of the procedure, plus the cost of medication.

Finally, there is the cost of death, assuming you choose a dignified one for your beloved. This varies with the size of the dog. For a fifty-pounder already dead, our vet charges $35 for cremation. If we bring in a live dog and are willing to take home the corpse, the cost is $45 for euthanasia. We pay $80 for euthanasia and cremation or $140 for euthanasia, cremation, plus return of the ashes, known as cremains, in a decorative canister.

Parnell:

Have Dog, Will Travel

A week into training at Guiding Eyes, Sue McCahill's pedestrian wake-up call over the dormitory loudspeaker system has been replaced with Craig Hedgecock blowing a funky reveille on his trumpet. Craig and Vargo are becoming a team, Sue says. He had wanted a big dog; when he was young, before he went blind, he had an Alaskan Malamute. Someone his size with his strength needs a hearty dog to match him in pace and pull. Vargo the big shepherd perfectly fills the bill. In fact, every one of the pairings has worked so far, although Bob Serrano is still having a hard time making the adjustment. In each class, Sue tells us, there are always some people that the trainers worry won't make it to graduation. Bob, who is so afraid of dogs, is high on their list of worries. They focus extra attention on him and Eagle, but he still often half jokes that he's just going to call a cab and go home. It isn't Eagle, his yellow lab, that's the problem, he confesses. It's just that he has never been close to any kind of dog. Petting Eagle, talking to him, relating to him is all new, as unfamiliar to Bob Serrano as learning to rely on a set of good canine eyes to make his way through the darkness of his world.

On Friday, January 17, the students go on their first field trip after a week of working the sidewalks of White Plains and Yorktown Heights. At 9:30 in the morning, they are escorted with their dogs into the cavernous interior of the Jefferson Valley Mall. At this hour, most of the stores aren't yet open, and although the mall is fairly unpopulated, its hallways rumble with echoing sounds of early-morning activity—a confusing landscape for people who have no sight to orient themselves. But they now have their dogs.

Cindy Blair has removed the rings from her fingers because she has a new harness and the stiff leather hurts her hands if the rings are on. Otherwise, she and Parnell look like they have been together forever. "He *is* a tiny guy," she says, "smaller than I expected. I sent out birth announcements the other day: *The Blair Family would like to announce the arrival of their newest member, Parnell.*

"I have no worries at all about him, but I am concerned about Brent's feelings. We are going to have to give him privileges that Parnell doesn't have around the house to make up for his having lost his responsibilities. But even so, it is going to be hard on Brent now that he is no longer a working guide dog. We can no longer take him to restaurants and into buildings where he's used to going. Now he'll be just a pet, while Parnell is the one who goes out on the town."

It is tough to help a retired dog cope with inactivity, but Cindy has done it once before, when her first guide dog, a large lab named Andrew, became too infirm to work and was replaced by Brent. "Your first guide dog is like your first love," Cindy says. "No matter what else happens, he is the one you never forget. The hardest thing I ever did was to write a letter to tell the puppy-raising family that Andrew had been put to sleep. He was fourteen years old."

Cindy is thrilled by the trip to the mall, although also frustrated. "Being here is killing me," she says. "I am a shopper. But they told us, 'no, no, you are here to work, not shop.' With Jessica Sanchez by their side, Cindy and Parnell walk past a store that sells handbags. "Oooo . . . leather!" Cindy cries with glee as she gets a good whiff.

"Now, show me what you can do," Jessica says when they approach an escalator. Parnell slows down as he was trained to do. "Feel the metal plate with your foot," Jessica tells Cindy. "Give Parnell a second to think about it. Feel the handrail bend, then start to walk." Cindy and Parnell hop on like old pros, the dog's soft pads narrowly but expertly escaping the gobbling metal steps. "Beautiful!" Jessica exclaims.

As Jessica and Sue walk alongside each student and the student's dog through the mall, including up and down the escalators, the other ten wait on some benches across from the Piercing Pavilion. Their dogs don't seem to particularly enjoy the echoing hallways of the mall, and they are more antsy than on a sidewalk. Craig's Vargo sniffs his way under the bench and gets his leash tangled up in a front leg, but he and Craig manage to undo the knot.

"May my child pet your dog?" a lady asks Bob Serrano.

Bob looks troubled. The idea that he now owns a dog seems odd enough, but he also has to remember the rules he was taught about educating the public politely when they want to play with his guide dog, and also remember to help keep his dog's mind on its task. "Well, he's not working just now," Bob says, considering the request. "That would be OK," he tells the lady. Eagle licks the young child as she pats the yellow fur on his broad head. "They told us to be diplomatic," Bob explains as the woman and her child walk away. "As long as your hand isn't on the harness, you can let them pet the dog. Otherwise, he is working." When the woman is gone, Bob reaches down to give Eagle a good solid pat on the shoulder, feeling cautiously as if he's not quite sure yet that the dog will still be there.

Etiquette for the Sighted

by Dorothy Harrison Eustis

Dorothy Harrison Eustis was a Philadelphia native who lived in Vevey, Switzerland, in the 1920s. There she bred and raised German Shepherds, many of which went on to become dependable working dogs for the Swiss Army, the Red Cross, and several European police forces. In the mid-1920s she visited a school in Potsdam, Germany, that was training shepherds to guide blinded war veterans and was so inspired by what she saw that she wrote "The Seeing Eye" for the Saturday Evening Post. *This story sparked the guide dog movement in America. Two years later, Mrs. Eustis wrote these "Ten Commandments" offering advice to the sighted who find themselves around a blind person and that person's guide dog.*

The public . . . allows itself to whistle, call and pet a blind leader and in so doing distracts it from its work perhaps at a most hazardous moment without realizing that the blind man is being momentarily deprived of his trained eyes. The dog in his newly found citizenship should be accorded the privileges of citizenship. As an illustration let me tell the story of a friend of mine who had one of my dogs. Getting into a trolley car one day with his dog he found her greeted by exclamations of delight and "Oh what a beautiful dog! Oh aren't you beautiful! Give me your paw," etc., etc., accompanied by pats and flattery.

Without a moment's hesitation he patted the lady on the shoulder and said, "You're a pretty little thing."

Consternation! Frigid atmosphere! The reply: "What do you mean by speaking to me? We've never been introduced!"

"Well, neither have you been introduced to my dog," was the perfectly reasonable answer!

For the education of the public the following commandments have been chosen.

1. Remember the leading dog is the eyes of the blind man first and a dog second.
2. Do not interfere in any way with either the leading dog or the blind master.
3. Do not speak to the dog at any time and under no circumstances call the name of the dog.
4. Do not touch or pet the dog.
5. Do not whistle to the dog or otherwise try to attract his attention, so diverting his mind from his work.
6. Do not feed the dog.
7. Do not shriek or exclaim as you pass the dog or meet him unexpectedly.
8. Give the opportunity for the dog to pass and do not willfully obstruct his way in order to see what he will do.
9. Speak to the master before touching him.
10. The blind master cannot protect himself or his dog. The dog can only protect himself and his master by a growl, this growl the public resents, therefore do not put the dog in a position where it is necessary for the dog to appear disagreeable.

In addition to Mrs. Eustis's ten points, Guiding Eyes for the Blind offers this advice to the sighted: "If you want to assist a person with a guide dog, first ask, 'May I help you?' If your offer is accepted, then offer your left elbow. Do not grab the guide dog, the leash, harness, or the person's arm. Doing so may place them in danger."

PARNELL:
THE VIRTUE
OF DISOBEDIENCE

The aptitude to disobey is the highest quality of a guide dog. Almost any pooch can learn to do what it is told; but a good guide dog also knows when to refuse a command. Morris Frank's book *The First Lady of the Seeing Eye* begins with his account of "the closest brush I have ever had with death," about the time Buddy refused to obey his "Forward!" command from a hotel hallway into an elevator. Mr. Frank was in a hurry, so when Buddy didn't budge, he dropped the harness and started forward alone. Buddy stepped ahead and stood in his path, preventing him from moving. At that moment a maid from somewhere behind him let out a scream. The elevator door was open, but the elevator wasn't there. Buddy had disobeyed his order to move forward. In doing so, she prevented him from falling into the elevator shaft and saved his life.

Many blind people have similar accounts of their dog's intelligent disobedience getting them out of a jam. Steve Kuusisto tells of the time Corky saved him from being run over by a Jeep. "It was my first week of training. I thought I was getting along pretty well, and I wanted to cross a street. I gave the command and Corky moved forward. But suddenly she stopped. I was impatient. I wanted to move. But she knew better. I could feel the rush of wind when that vehicle sped past just in front of us. At that moment, I understood what it was all about. Trust. Our bond had been formed."

To help students develop that trust, Sue and Jessica have them cross busy streets in Yorktown Heights. When that works out well, they tell them to walk around the Guiding Eyes campus, crossing driveways and the parking lot. Assistant trainers get behind the wheels of cars and drive as if they plan to run over the blind people. The well-trained dogs take care of them every time; and as they do, the students learn to depend on their dogs the way sighted people depend on their vision.

"To be a guide dog is like being a traffic controller at an airport," Steve Kuusisto says. "What makes a good one is the ability to shoulder so much responsibility and be one hundred percent reliable. Ninety-nine percent isn't good enough. The dog must watch everything: the street, the traffic flow, that car running a red light, a double-parked car that starts to move. It has to be aware of all those things simultaneously . . . then be able to go into the Metropolitan Opera among hundreds of milling people and stay perfectly calm and quiet under the seat for three hours. Add to all that external pressure the fact that the dog is working with a person who may be frightened, uncertain, and insecure."

To test their confidence two days before graduation, the twelve students and their dogs go into New York City to walk along midtown streets, take buses and subways, negotiate crowded department stores, and find their way onto elevators and escalators in strange buildings.

While Sue McCahill and some of the students are on a crosstown bus, a blind woman with a German Shepherd steps on. Somehow, Sue instantly recognizes the dog as one from Fidelco, an organization in Bloomfield, Connecticut, that trains dogs for the blind; and when the blind lady realizes that the bus has a large population of novices with their dogs, she panics. She is worried Alison Dolan's yellow lab Colleen will pick a fight. "Nonsense," Alison tells her, annoyed that the woman has so little faith in the Guiding Eyes dogs. The crowded city bus jolts along its route and the blind people are confronted with more unexpected and troublesome behavior. A sighted woman seated near Alison finds it fun to poke Alison's dog Colleen in the nose with a pointed finger from the time she sits down to the time the bus reaches her stop. But Colleen is cool; so is Alison.

"This is the Looney Toon bus!" Tom Massa declares.

"Please!" Craig jokes back. "The 'Mentally Challenged Bus,' not 'Looney Toon.' " Craig, a social worker who says he has "seen it all," is in a great mood. Later, as he and Vargo stroll the aisle of a midtown record store, a woman approaches, bends down toward the German Shepherd, and says, "Hi, Sweety, you're so cute."

"Thank you very much," Craig replies in a flirty voice. "You are pretty cute yourself."

Flustered, the woman scurries away. To a far greater degree than they ever experienced during their work in the suburban Yorktown Heights area (where local residents are quite accustomed to seeing Guiding Eyes pupils navigating the sidewalks), students are now learning a new code of social etiquette necessary when you travel with a dog. "Everyone will want to pet your dog." Steve Kuusisto warns. "And you don't want to be rude to them. But you simply have to tell them that your dog is busy. Your dog is *working*. Sometimes, what I want to say to them when they insist on treating Corky like any pet is, 'Dog! What dog?! They gave me a dog???' And on occasion, I tell them that her name is Jasper or something else I make up on the spot. So they call, 'Hi Jasper,' and she pays no attention to them."

Having a dog working with you presents some hazards, but it also creates social opportunities. Several students note how different it is to walk along the street with a dog as compared to a white cane. Aside from speed and security, a dog sparks people's interest and encourages familiarity. "They avoided me when I walked with a cane," one student recalls. "No one wants to talk to the blind man. Now, everybody wants to know about my dog."

Even the tentative Bob Serrano acknowledges the difference. "I have enough vision to see people part like the Red Sea when I walk Eagle along the sidewalk," he says. "They sure didn't do that when I had a cane. I've had my cane knocked out of my hand by cars. But with the dog, people are different. Everything is different! To move along a crowded sidewalk is like surfing." When you see Bob make his way through the pedestrian traffic with Eagle in the lead at the end of his harness taking cues and letting Bob know about every obstacle in his path, it is hard to believe that three weeks ago Bob didn't think he would make it through the program, and it is impossible to think that he hasn't worked closely with a dog most of his life.

Cindy Blair does so well in New York with Parnell that she is frustrated by the fast trip through Bloomingdale's, which allows the students no time to buy anything. So the next day, a free day before the official graduation ceremony, she hops a Guiding Eyes van and "free-lances" at the Jefferson Valley Mall. It is only her second time at the mall, after that initiation walk-through in the morning, but Cindy was savvy enough to make note of where all the interesting stores were. She finds the tobacconist and buys a cigar that says *It's a Girl* for Spencer McMillan, a shy fellow classmate from Colorado whose wife, back home, just had a baby. She buys a sweatshirt for her teenage son, a key chain for her husband, and doggy toys for Parnell and Brent—match-ing bones they can both gnaw and a Booda rope for Brent to toss around while Parnell is working. She buys nothing at The Gap, despite Parnell's insistence on taking her right to the front door. "This must have been Jessica's favorite place to shop," Cindy surmises.

She is eager to know everything about her new canine partner. "The other day I found out that he fetched," she says in a mischie-vous tone of voice. "The trainers specifically forbade us from trying anything like that yet, but I was so curious. So my sneaker 'acciden-tally' came off my foot and I 'accidentally' kicked it across the room. He went after it like a shot and brought it right back to me. The only problem was, I didn't know the command to get him to release it. I heard Jessica coming up the stairs and I didn't want her to see Parnell with a shoe in his mouth—that's a real no-no—so I started hollering every release command I know—'drop it!' . . . 'release!' . . . finally, I said, 'Leave it!' and he put the shoe in my hand. I quickly got it on my foot before Jessica came in. It was all slimy from his mouth, but she never knew." The more she gets to know Parnell, the more Cindy wants to know about him. "I want to meet his family," she says. "I want to find out what he was like. Did he live in a city? Has he been in a home with children? Look at him," she says, petting the little black lab as he lies with all four legs stretched out on the cool mall floor. "He lies down like a frog. I wonder if they know about that?"

Cindy's pairing with Parnell is a success in large part because Par-nell was taught so well in his formative puppy years. Diligent, serene, alert, and caring, he is an example of the canine species at its finest. He is a dog to make those who bred and raised him proud.

CLEMENTINE:
THE END OF OUR ROPE

After a year living with our new puppy, we were not proud. We had changed thanks to our relationship with Clementine, and the change was not for the better. For one thing, we never invited guests to our house anymore. We used to be quite social and now it was just too hard to have company. We imagined the horrified looks on people's faces as we attempted to host an evening meal only to interrupt conversations by screaming "NO!" when Clementine did something awful, or if we segregated her in the ex-pen it would be impossible to get through dinner without one or both of us jumping up from the table every six seconds to make sure she wasn't chewing her bedding or to tell her to stop barking.

We had run out of options. We had done all we knew how to do. The expensive valerian root tranquilizer we bought at the health food store and the kava root, which both promised to mellow her out did nothing, nor did the massage book for pets we tried. She liked all the little circles and rubdowns we did up and down her beefy legs and chest but as soon as we stopped she was up and running. We were exhausted and frustrated, and feeling more and more isolated in our dogcentric dilemma. We knew we had to get back on track and try to live normal lives despite our idiotic pet. After all, she was not a dangerous dog, not even an evil one. She was just a huge, out-of-control nudnik growing in strength and size by the minute.

We were beginning to hit the wall of our own limitations. We had done our best and when that failed we had called in experts. We had done the drills and walked the walk and nothing was working. We could feel an ennui set in, a deep exhaustion brought on by repeated failures, and we were experiencing the soft, sinking feeling of giving up.

Our house was a mess, with stacks of how-to-train-a-dog books piled up on the tables, the counters were covered with herbs and sprays and collars that had done nothing to alleviate the behavior. We had done what we could and were slowly being smothered by our huge inability to change Clementine's behavior. We figured that our only hope of regaining some normalcy was to change our own behavior.

PARNELL:

GRADUATION DAY

On a Saturday morning nearly four weeks after arriving in York-town Heights, local florists deliver bouquets to the Guiding Eyes school, many of them sent by the puppy-raising families, others by friends and families of the graduates. The flowers are placed in the hallways, their cards displayed for the sighted to see. *To Carl and New Friend* one says. *Good Luck Dutchess* says another, referring to Rosario Cura's black lab.

Lunch in the school dining room is a festive meal: a flap of white-meat turkey draped on a pile of bread stuffing and covered with gravy, accompanied by candied yams and broccoli with pink ice cream for dessert. In anticipation, several of the students are already dressed for the ceremonies—men in ties and pressed shirts, women in special-occasion dresses. As on any graduation day, spirits are high. But these students are especially excited, for in just a short while they will at long last be meeting the families who raised their dogs.

After lunch, students take their dogs back to the dorm rooms so the animals can make a ceremonial entrance during the official pro-ceedings. Meanwhile, the hallways begin to fill up with puppy rais-ing families, friends, trainers, graduates, and a few retired guide dogs who have returned as honored alumni. It is a celebration scene, as convivial as a bright spring morning at a church door, with everyone wearing their Sunday best. Trainers and students who have worn nothing but jeans and sweat clothes for the last three weeks are now in pretty dresses, high heels, suits and ties.

"It is so important to the people who get the dogs that we puppy raisers be here today," says Mary Jane Gibbons of North Carolina, who raised Moseley and wears a five-puppy medallion on her collar to indicate how many dogs she has guided into adulthood for the Guiding Eyes program. "They want to know everything about their dog. So I brought a little photo album." Many puppy raisers bring photo albums, unfazed by any apparent incongruity of showing pictures to a blind person. Even if the blind people cannot see the images, they can hear the emotions in a puppy raiser's voice when important moments and beloved people are pointed out in the album; and the dogs' new masters readily avow that they treasure these images that they will never see.

Mary Jane Gibbons has not yet met Moseley's new master, Murry Dimon, but to anyone who expresses interest, she shows the album filled with baby pictures of Moseley when he was a chubby puppy. "This was his going-away party," she says, pointing to a picture of the happy black lab surrounded by loving people. There is a picture of Moseley with a flower in his mouth, one of Moseley draped across her cousin, who is lying on the couch. "Oh, this is bad," she says with no disapprobation whatsoever in her voice. "They wouldn't like it if they knew I let him get on top of somebody. . . . Here is a picture of Moseley's brother. . . . Here he is in the Christmas parade in Waynesville, wearing his guide-dog-in-Pretraining coat [precursor to a harness, and a way of alerting to the public that he is a service dog in training]. . . . Here is a picture of Moseley with the staff at the veterinarian's office. . . . This is Moseley sleeping. . . . This is a picture of Dr. Moseley, after whom he was named. . . . [Mary Jane reminds onlookers that Moseley came from outside the G.E.B. breeding program.] This is Moseley posing with the manager of the local McDonald's. Everybody loves him. He was so laid-back as a puppy. He was so, so good. All my friends and all the other puppy raisers I know grew so sick of me always saying how perfect he was. It was so hard to let him go. But I knew he would be happier with something to do. When it came time to give him up, I couldn't bear to put him on the plane, so I drove him up here myself."

As Ms. Gibbons brags about the dog she raised with unconcealed love and affection, its trainer, Jessica Sanchez—Moseley's greatest fan—walks past. She grabs the album, pores over it with greedy eyes that fill with tears at all the images of Moseley as a pup. "You raised an angel," she sobs.

By one o'clock the Campbell Lounge is packed, standing room only, with an overflow crowd gathered just outside the glass doors on the quadrangle grass. Throughout the rows of folding chairs packed with people are dogs squeezed in underneath the seats—some working for their blind masters, some retired. At the front of the room, a row of empty chairs faces the audience. The ceremony begins when the class of twelve students is led into the room, each with their dog, and they take their seats.

In keeping with the spirit of this ceremony occurring on Superbowl Weekend, William Badger, CEO of Guiding Eyes, greets the audience wearing a hat in the shape of a wedge of cheese, the kind Green Bay Packers fans wear. Badger appears to be a corporate type, a man in well-cut clothes with perfectly barbered hair and regular features. The cheese is incongruous on his formal head, but it bespeaks the soul of his institution, which, despite all its good work, never seems sanctimonious. "I am the big cheese around here," he jokes to break the ice. And strangely, somehow, all twelve blind students crack up laughing at the visual joke. Apparently someone has told them about the hat; and their laughter reassures all assembled that they are very much part of the room.

Hat removed, Badger begins the program with a parable about an old man who is walking along the ocean shore one night after a big storm has washed thousands of starfish up onto the sand. The old man is throwing them back into the water, one by one, to save them from death when the sun rises. A small boy asks him why he is bothering to do this; how can he make a difference? The man picks up a starfish and throws it in the water. He tells the boy, "For that starfish, I made a difference." Badger knows that no one has come to hear him speak. So he quickly turns the spotlight on the twelve graduates.

Alison Dolan stands to give the class speech. She describes the last three weeks as "an overwhelming, life-changing experience." Of her first solo walk, she says, "That was the first time in years that I had walked by myself since I lost my vision. I felt free." By the end of her talk, there are many sniffles in the room—from sighted and blind people alike. When she sits, applause rings out. Craig Hedgecock's German Shepherd Vargo lets loose with an enthusiastic round of barks.

Each student stands and says what's on their mind. For many of the puppy raisers, it is their first opportunity to see and hear the person to whom their dog went.

"Victor is very low-key," Esther Acha says to the group. "The first thing I noticed is that his tail is not a coffee table killer."

"Mmm-hmmm!" someone who obviously knows her yellow lab in the crowd agrees.

"Watch me!" Cindy says when she stands with Parnell by her side. "Now I can fly. I will soar like an eagle."

Dan and Susan Fisher-Owens, who have driven up from their current residence in Washington, DC, sit with their retired guide dog Matthew at their feet and crane their necks to have a look at Parnell as Cindy speaks. They beam with pride. Susan is wearing earrings in the shape of black Labrador Retrievers.

"Dutchess is like me," high-schooler Rosie Cura says of her black lab. "When I turn on the light in the morning, she covers her eyes. She doesn't like to get up. I have to share my stuffed rabbit with her, but we've worked that out. She gets it one night, I get it the next."

"Moseley is a clown," Murry Dimon tells the crowd. "He was off his tie-down in my room and I felt around and suddenly he was gone. I thought, *How can I lose a ninety-four-pound dog in one small bedroom?* I was about to call Jessica when I found him hiding in the closet." Hiding in a closet is by no means correct guide dog behavior, but the room roars with laughter at the story; and Mary Jane Gibbons, who knows Moseley's slightly quirky personality better than anyone, is teary-eyed remembering his antics as a growing puppy.

Each student's little account of life with the new dog is welcomed by applause. The clapping stirs up Vargo and he joins the cheers by barking enthusiastically. "I am a musician," Craig Hedgecock says. "I guess he is, too."

"Eli is a real get-around-town kind of guy," Tom Massa tells the audience. "I think they did a good job of matching us up."

When Henry Tucker stands, he says, "I thank Guiding Eyes for helping me retire my cane."

Bob Serrano is overcome with emotion when it is his turn to speak. "When I first came," he stammers, "I wanted to run back home. I didn't think I was going to make it"—tears are pouring down his cheeks—"But I did make it!"

Sue McCahill, sitting in the front row, is crying, too, with joy. "Yes you did!" she yells loud enough for the whole room to hear. "You made it, Bob!" The room cheers his success as Vargo joins them with a flurry of barks and happy howls.

Head trainer Kathy Zubrycki stands before the assembled group. One by one she introduces the puppy-raising families and tells them in what city and state their puppies will now be residing. From each family, a representative rises and receives a certificate, then goes to shake hands with the person who got their dog. In return, the blind person hands them the formal portrait.

The Waters Family of Fort Ann, New York, and Genie Christiansen of Essex, Vermont, are announced as being the ones who raised Esther Acha's Victor. Esther, who is wearing a glittering brocade gown from Lane Bryant, is pouring tears and quivering with emotion. A woman from the audience puts a pile of tissue in her hands so she can blot her face.

At the conclusion of the ceremony, two assistant trainers carry out a pair of fuzzy-furred seven-week-old puppies, one black lab, one yellow lab, and show them to the crowd. They are available for adoption, to be raised for the program. Among this dog-loving group, the sight of the puppies provokes great moans of adoration and joy, and after the ceremony, experienced families eager for new puppies consult with members of the staff and arrange to bring one home.

When the formalities have finished, graduates and puppy raisers have a party in the common rooms and hallways of the school. Cake and coffee and soft drinks are set out in the cafeteria. It is a strange sort of affair, for so much socializing takes place about eighteen inches off the ground, at dog level, where the original families can once again cuddle the pups they raised and tell the new masters all about them. Cindy is sitting on a chair with Parnell stretched out froglike on the cool linoleum in front of her. When Sue and Dan come by to introduce themselves, Parnell's ears perk up. When he spots his old buddy Matthew, he shudders with ecstasy, wiggling tip to toe. The two old friends sniff each other everywhere as Susan and Dan introduce themselves to Cindy.

Susan begins to tell of Parnell's life—his reaction to the first summer's heat, his residency at Johns Hopkins, his award as the student most likely to devote himself to public service. "I'll warn you," she tells Cindy, "he loves water. One day on the way to school, he rolled in mud, I mean really rolled until he became a chocolate lab. I didn't have anything to clean him, but I ran into a maintenance man who knew how to open a hydrant on the street. He turned it on. Parnell stuck his head in the water and wouldn't take it out. People walked past us, amazed."

Cindy is drinking in every detail about Parnell's life, eager for more.

Dan's father and mother come by with cameras to record the occasion. "Oh, it's so nice to see Parney again," Dan's father says.

"Did you feed him table food?" Cindy asks.

"Never," Dan says.

"I could tell," Cindy says. "Thank you! . . . You know, he likes to steal the covers off my bed."

"I know," Dan says. "He loves to sleep with others. He slept with Matthew. And sometimes he would nap with me."

As Dan and Cindy discuss the fine points of Parnell's personality, Susan Fisher-Owens takes a friend aside to confide a story that she says she wouldn't dare tell to a dog recipient on graduation day, for fear it might upset her. "Later," Susan says. "Once she's settled, I can tell her about the time Parnell was young and we got some superabsorbent litter for the cat's box. Well, Parnell went in there for a big helping of 'cat brownies,' and the litter stuck to his face, to his lips, and inside his mouth. We had to use a high-powered hose to get it off."

"He's on three cups of food in the morning and three at night," Cindy tells Dan.

"That sounds about right," Dan says. "He had bad dandruff when he started, so we switched foods around and it cleared up."

"He's great at park time," Cindy says. "Does his business first of all the other dogs."

"He was always that way," Dan says, "At least after that first hot summer. Matthew, he's different," he says, patting the twelve-year-old yellow lab on the head and straightening his jaunty green bandanna. "He always needed more supervision."

"Do you know what Parnell's favorite game is?" Sue asks Cindy. "It's Chase Me. But he is unidirectional, only from one end of the apartment to the other. Then we walk back and start over again. He also used to love pulling me around in my desk chair."

"He's got a sweet spot for women," Dan notes. "He always was a mama's boy."

CLEMENTINE:
GRUDGE MATCH

In an attempt to feel normal again despite our year of puppy hell, we invited close friends for dinner one evening. These were people we knew who loved dogs and would understand the chaos they were about to experience. Jane was going about the task of baking a layer cake, and Michael was out shopping for other parts of the meal.

It was 10 A.M., the apex of Clementine's worst morning behavior. She was already pacing, yelping, scratching at the kitchen door to go out, then instantly scratching to come back in. Lewis was perched warily atop her cage and Minerva had made herself scarce, hiding somewhere upstairs, as Clementine bounced from place to place like a pinball in a million-point game.

To distract herself, Jane turned on the small kitchen television as she separated egg whites for the cake. Self-help guru John Bradshaw was giving a lecture on the public television station. He was a good antidote to Clementine—calm, gentle, easy to listen to. As Jane cooked, she sopped up his beneficent words, nodding in agreement with his philosophy of finding inner peace and family harmony.

It was a difficult cake recipe, and Jane was trying to pay attention to the details as Clementine started marching around the kitchen with the inside doormat in her mouth, "Stop that! Sit!" Jane called out by rote.

Clementine paid no attention whatsoever. She dropped the door-mat and stood on her hind legs and pulled a kitchen towel off the rack, barking when Jane ignored her.

Jane turned up the volume on the television to drown out the barking.

Frustrated at being ignored, Clementine latched on to the hem of Jane's long cotton prairie skirt.

"Get off me!" Jane yelled. Skirt tug-of-war was at the top of the Not Allowed list. It had to be stopped because if a dog got away with that, it was the first step on the road to serious aggression. With all puppies we owned we never played tug-of-war even as a game. Any authority in canine behavior will tell you that it is never a good idea to instigate any contest where you and your dog challenge each other in a contest of wills or of strength, and until Clementine, this admonition was never a problem. We had never had to discourage a tug-of-war between a dog and our clothing . . . especially with us in it.

Undaunted, Clementine backed up, skirt in mouth, eyes blazing with glee. Because this was the most taboo game of all, it was also the best.

Jane reached down to grab Clementine's collar, but before she got hold of it, she heard a loud ripping sound. With one good yank, Clementine had torn the calico skirt from hem to waist.

The sound of the fabric tearing was the launch code for an emotional nuke. The silo doors had opened; the rocket engines rumbled; the apocalypse was at hand. Jane swiveled and stared down at the dog. Instinctively, Clementine knew the game had taken a deadly turn; a point of no return had been crossed. She dropped the fabric from her mouth. Her jaw went slack.

"You stupid, idiotic asshole!" Jane screamed, lunging toward the stunned dog. With one arm flying in Clementine's direction, the other hand accidentally hit the china bowl on the counter, sending a dozen slimy egg yolks onto the floor. An open box of cake flour at the edge of the counter joined the cascade. Jane grabbed at Clementine's collar, and as she bucked and jumped and tried to get away, they both slid wildly across the floor, skating and slipping in a mucky sea of eggs and flour.

Clementine had been yelled at endlessly before but she had learned to toss it off as no real threat.

Now she was face-to-face with a seriously angry alpha wolf, a wolf in human clothing wearing a ripped cowgirl skirt with eggs and flour clinging to her skin and bits of broken china sticking to that. Hyperventilating hard enough to drown out John Bradshaw's soothing tones, Jane was not thinking anymore. She was doing. *"You will stop this shit, and you will behave yourself!"* she screamed at the top of her lungs.

Clementine struggled and broke free. Jane chased her around the center island of the kitchen, toppling over cake pans and a large box of laundry detergent, which spilled on the floor as they zoomed by.

Jane grabbed Clementine's back leg and held tight. They skidded on the detergent pebbles and crashed headfirst into a china cabinet. Clementine was struggling like mad to get away, but Jane knew that if she lost this contest, it would be all over. It had come down to this very ugly moment: Either Jane or Clementine would walk away as top dog. Jane, who usually thinks of herself as a somewhat meek and fearful person, knew she had to reach deep inside to the most primal part of her being and give all her strength to the struggle rather than back off.

It was a clash of titans. Jane is a big woman, and Clementine, although still technically a puppy, was now 128 pounds of lean muscled dog. Jane got an arm around Clementine's shoulders and dropped down on top of her. She was going to turn this dog on her back and make her submit. The thud of their bodies sent a vase filled with flowers bought for the dinner party crashing down on the kitchen tiles. Water flowed all around as Jane and Clementine continued grappling.

With superhuman strength generated by a year of puppy hell, Jane flipped Clementine on her back and straddled her chest, squatting atop her like a professional wrestler. She held her forearm forcefully at Clementine's throat hard enough to make the dog know that Jane now held the power of life and death over her. There were no more words or commands left to issue. Jane and Clementine were communicating in the most elemental animal language.

Every taut muscle in Clementine's body went limp. She issued a primal moan and stayed very still, and one last time, she peed where she wasn't supposed to pee. Her bladder emptying was the white flag of surrender, ultimate submission. The room was completely silent except for John Bradshaw's honey rich voice on the television and the sound of dog and human breath coming hard and fast. Jane could hear her own racing heartbeat, and feel Clementine's as well. For the first time ever, they were in synch.

When Michael returned with the groceries, Jane was standing in her underpants mopping up eggs, flour, pee, detergent, and shards of china with what was left of her skirt. "We better rethink dessert," she said.

"What happened here?" Michael asked, looking shocked. "Where's Clementine?"

Clementine had retreated to her dog bed, and after making an elaborate ritual of pawing and arranging the fabric, had settled herself down in a tight circle where she spent the rest of the day, immobile. She regarded us warily with her eyes bigger than ever. She got up exactly twice, one time to eat, another to go outside. Each time, she quickly returned to her bed, an island of safety.

The dinner party went rather smoothly. Clementine's presence was hardly noticed, but one guest did remark about the shell-shocked look on Jane's face. Jane tossed off an excuse about PMS or some such thing, still unable to digest what had happened in the kitchen that morning, much less discuss it.

The next day Clementine was still subdued. Minerva felt brave enough to take a stroll over and sniff at her cautiously. Only the tip of Clementine's tail wagged.

We rewarded her peaceful attitude. We sat by her bed and stroked her ears and talked gently to her. In a few days, she returned to her basic energetic self, but she was different. When we said "Go to your place," she went there, and she stayed.

As with Clementine, it took Jane a few days to recover. She realized that what she had done could have had disastrous results if Clementine had been a vicious creature instead of an out-of-control pest. With a truly mean dog of Clementine's size and weight, such a confrontation might easily have left Jane dead on the kitchen floor.

Because of this very real threat, we would never recommend Jane's kamikaze approach to dog training to anyone. We were lucky. For all her unruliness, Clementine is at heart a totally benign creature, and possibly we were veterans of enough puppy-raising campaigns to know this. Jane had unconsciously trusted her instinct to push the envelope to the point she did, but again, every dog is different. And again: we were lucky.

Of course it is possible that if Clementine's behaviors had been allowed to continue a few more years or even months, she indeed might have become aggressive instead of pesty. We are glad that we did what it took to stop the skirt tugging and her other dominant behavior while she was young enough to change.

The one sure lesson we learned from this confrontation is that anything you do to make a puppy behave must come from the heart. Like children, dogs are geniuses in psyching out their "parents" and detecting a halfhearted *no* from a real one. We have all heard parents say "Johnny, get off that couch" a dozen times, and little Johnny continues to jump on the couch until the parent gets to a certain level of true exasperation, and says the exact same words again but this time MEANS IT. Then Johnny gets off the couch. Clementine was a more hardheaded puppy than most we have raised, but in retrospect we now see that we had grown complacent in our puppy-raising skills, and while we were going through all the right motions, we were less mentally focused than we had been when we were younger and more enthusiastic about really working with a puppy.

In time we were also gifted with a genetic overview that helped explain some of Clementine's behavior. Debby Vargas reported that Clementine's litter mates were far more boisterous then the usual Bullmastiffs, and that one of the males had learned to "climb trees." Even if this is a slight exaggeration, it is still an eye-opening statement about a breed that is not normally known for its rambunctious behavior. It shows that even within one breed there can be a wide range of personality. Our previous four Bullmastiffs had come from a different kennel and descended from more placid specimens.

We also learned (once our heads cleared of the pink cloud of Sam infatuation) that Clementine's father was a bit of a hard case himself when it came to housebreaking. At age five he still liked to spray Mimi's couches or chairs when he walked by them. We always thought that Mimi was more forgiving then we are with dogs, but we have since accepted the fact that nature is at least as potent a force as nurture in raising a puppy.

PARNELL:

GOING HOME

The day after the graduation ceremony at Guiding Eyes for the Blind in Yorktown Heights, retreads go home. Novice dog owners remain at the school another week for additional training to help them cope with whatever unique situations their lives might present their dog: plane travel, crowds, hours of patient inactivity while their master doesn't need guiding. Those who have never owned a dog must be taught certain basic routines that every good pet owner needs to know: grooming (minimal for Labrador Retrievers), regular health checks, and food preferences.

Even those blind people who are familiar with pet care need to be reminded of the difference between a pet and a working dog. Guide dogs have been programmed to thrive on a fairly regimented life: feedings at a regular hour, predictable periods of R&R, and a high expectation of responsible behavior. When students take new dogs home, they are told not to let any other family member play with it, walk it, or give it orders, at least at first. Their primary goal should be to get the dog to focus entirely on them, not anyone else. It is furthermore expected that at least for the first few weeks the dog should spend the night in its master's bedroom on a tie-down (as it did at the school). This minimizes wandering and household accidents, and further reinforces the lifeline connection between dog and master. Later, when the tie-down is eliminated and the dog is given run of the house, a majority of guide dogs choose to make their special place a spot in the master's bedroom.

For retread Cindy Blair and her new dog, Parnell, a trip home means seven hours on the train. "My husband informed me that because I was coming home on Superbowl Sunday, I'd have to take a cab from the station," Cindy laughs. "But I do look forward to the train ride. That is seven hours' bonding time for me and the Parnster."

Cindy carefully orchestrates Parnell's arrival Sunday night. Although she knows that she and only she should be with Parnell during these first moments of their togetherness at home, she hands Parnell's leash to her husband before she even gets to the front door so he can take the new dog into the backyard and play with him there. Cindy has Brent's feelings to think about. She doesn't want to walk into the house after a month away and have Brent see her in the company of another, younger dog. So when she enters, she enters alone. Brent sniffs and licks her and wags his tail with joy. After she and her old guide say a long hello, she tells him, "Brent, I want you to come meet your new friend." She leads the veteran to the doors that open into the backyard. Parnell enters, curious and cautious. The two dogs—both professionals well trained to deal with any circumstances—give each other a good once-over, then relax and sit side by side at Cindy's feet, waiting to work.

Later that night, Parnell is allowed to explore the house at his leisure. At bedtime, the two dogs sleep on either side of the bed in the master bedroom.

Monday morning at eight o'clock, Brent whines when the harness comes out and Cindy doesn't put it on him. He pushes his way close to her, sitting obediently at her feet. But all he can do is watch her put the harness on Parnell and walk out the door with her new guide. As she swiftly moves along the sidewalk toward the bus stop, Cindy herself is crying.

She boards the bus and Parnell guides her into downtown Rochester for coffee with a friend. Parnell takes her into a big office building, across busy streets, into elevators and up and down escalators. "It is like we've been a team for years," Cindy declares. "It is like he just slid into my life. And he fits perfectly." When her friends meet him, they comment on how good he looks paired with her: both dog and master are dapper characters with a bouyant mien, and he soon begins to sport a bandanna to match what she is wearing when they go out on the town.

Parnell is flawless his first day on the job, but Cindy makes one mistake. She was so thrilled to have her new dog that when she left her house in the morning, she did not landmark it—a basic technique of stopping and pulling on the harness a few times to let a dog know that this is a significant destination, a place to stop or turn. So when she and Parnell return from town, the diligent guide dog walks right past her house and continues moving forward, having no sense yet of where he lives. By the end of the block, Cindy realizes that Parnell will continue walking forever. He needs her to tell him where to turn in. So she directs him back to the place he will soon know as home. That night, she calls her friends at Guiding Eyes—the first-timers who had stayed for an extra week of training—and warns them, "Whatever you do when you get home, landmark your house!"

The next day, Cindy landmarks the crossing at the nearby railroad tracks, and the day after that she takes him to her son's school, where she has PTA business to attend to. Parnell's upbringing at Johns Hopkins serves him well. He is entirely comfortable negotiating hallways and classrooms.

One morning well into Parnell's tenure as her guide dog, Cindy clips on the harness and walks outside. About two houses down, she begins to feel that something is wrong. Parnell isn't going well at all. He is pulling and tugging. Then Cindy realizes what has happened. She has put the harness on Brent rather than on Parnell, and Brent once again is flinching when her cues gall his tender skin. Somehow, that old dog managed to figure out a way to get Parnell far from the front door where he normally waits when he knows Cindy is going out. "Brent didn't say a thing when I put the harness on him, just the way I used to do," Cindy says. "He knew he had me fooled." Later, she buys a different collar for Brent so she can feel who's who and Brent can never play that trick again.

Still, Brent always waits by the door, hoping against hope that this time Cindy will take him out into the world and let him be her eyes instead of the young newcomer. But Brent's days in a harness are definitely over. Not that there aren't good compensations for being retired. Parnell, the working dog, is never allowed on the furniture. Brent can sleep in bed. "That is a privilege of his retirement," Cindy proclaims. "But once he got used to it, he started gloating by hanging his head over the side of the bed and lording his status over Parnell. That's not fair, so now he is not allowed to hang off the side where Parnell can see him."

As Parnell has settled into his work life, the Blair family has come to know new facets of his personality. "It took me some time to realize how much Parnell likes to play," Cindy says. "He is so good at his work, but he likes his fun, too. One of his great pleasures, they have discovered, is dancing. Cindy's fifteen-year-old son Michael kneels down so Parnell can put both paws on his shoulders. Parnell kisses Michael, who then stands up and waltzes around the room, paw-in-arm with the happy black lab.

At home, when he is not in his harness, Parnell doesn't go anywhere without his Stuffy toy—a sort of gingerbread man with sheep fleece. He carries it around with him and he sleeps with it. "Oh, how he hates it when I clean that toy," Cindy says. "He sits by the dryer waiting for it to come out. And the first thing he does, when it is still warm, is to rub it all around on the floor so it gets dirty again. We recently bought two backup Stuffies just in case something happens to this one. We're going to do everything we can to see to it that Parnell is happy. He deserves it."

When the Blairs open their backyard pool, it becomes apparent that Parnell yearns to go swimming. Of course he does—water is many labs' favorite element; and Cindy recalls Susan Fisher-Owens' story of Parnell putting his head in the spray from the fire hydrant when he was a pup. But because it is an above-ground pool, the Blairs worry that an errant claw could tear the sides and flood their yard. So Parnell gets his own pool: a little "Mr. Turtle" wading tub designed for children, complete with floating rubber balls and inflatable boat. He is in ecstasy; and every morning when he goes into the backyard at 6 A.M., his first order of business is to find the garden hose and drag it to the pool, hinting to his family that he'd like it filled.

Parnell learns to relish watching baseball. At young Michael's encouragement, Cindy and Parnell join him at day games played in Rochester's minor league stadium where, Cindy boasts, "The handicapped seats are the best!" Sitting with Cindy and Michael just above the boxes between home plate and first place, Parnell watches every move on the field. Teenage Michael is especially pleased with the dog's company, at the ball game and elsewhere around town, because he soon discovers that the handsome, brown-eyed, eighty-seven-pound hunk is what he calls a chick magnet. "Beautiful girls are always stopping by to pet the nice dog," Cindy says. "Parnell has something women can't resist—and I confirmed this with the Fisher-Owenses, who said he always was a ladies' man—so my son sits there and gives them permission to pet *his* dog. 'Mom,' he whispers, 'Move aside.' "

Cindy is most amazed by The Parn Man's strict adherence to the rules as he has learned them. Off-duty, he loves to splash gaily in his pool and even to coax some play from Brent (whom he still respects as the senior dog around the house), but when Parnell is in harness, nothing can distract him or weaken his resolve to do his job. If Cindy is with a group of people and the others jay-walk across the street, Parnell refuses to follow. Instead, he leads Cindy to the crosswalk. "He will not take a shortcut," Cindy says. "So it might take me a few extra minutes to get somewhere, but I don't mind because I know I am safe. I have gone farther with him than with any other dog, so far that my family bought me a cell phone to keep in touch. Parnell has such an incredible sense of duty that I have never once had to discipline him. He is too good to be true. Sometimes, I wait for that other paw to fall . . . but I don't believe it ever will."

Cindy comes to believe fully in Parnell on Easter Sunday. That day, the two of them go to church early in the morning for a children's breakfast party. A sixteen-year-old friend of Cindy's son Michael is playing the part of the Easter Bunny, outfitted in a full body costume with big ears, floppy feet, and pompom tail. Parnell knows the boy well, but when he sees a six-foot-tall bunny saunter into the room, ears up and whiskers akimbo, he is flabbergasted. No experiences he had during his Guiding Eyes education quite prepared him for an encounter with a gigantic rodent that moves like a man. Parnell backs up and barks, a natural reaction in any animal confronted by a big, scary alien. But he doesn't run, nor does he attack. After a short stand-off between gigantic rabbit and dog, Parnell's well-honed instincts steady him; months of expert training offer further reassurance. Just as he did when he was seven weeks old and overcame his shock at the snapped-opened umbrella and the rattling can full of coins, just as he did when Russ Post shot the .32 pistol in the air at the In-For-Training tests, Parnell assesses the situation and decides he can deal with it. Panic fading, he cautiously approaches the huge rabbit; and finally, when he is close enough for a good sniff, he gets the nice, reassuring scent of the boy he knows. His tail wags. He can relax because he is safe . . . and because he knows his Cindy is safe, too.

CLEMENTINE:
THE ANNIVERSARY GIFT

It would be nice to conclude the saga of Clementine's first two years by saying that she has turned into a model canine citizen. In truth she has remained very much herself, but a much more pleasant version than she once was. Physically she is still smaller than her litter mates and to Mimi Einstein's dismay, she still has a white stripe in the middle of her head. She is a bully little tank of a dog with an almost comically expressive face. Now when we issue a command her eyes widen and she looks momentarily dumbfounded as if the devil is whispering into one ear, an angel into the other. And she has to wait out the raging debate before she remembers what it is she is supposed to do.

She is ninety-five percent housebroken, and she can actually walk past an open bathroom door without chewing the roll of toilet paper off the wall fixture. She is capable of sitting still for a good long while without pacing, and she mostly leaves Minerva and Lewis in peace. Need we say that she absolutely never tugs on Jane's skirt?

As always, she is a very affectionate girl. She is not happy unless she sits as close to us as possible. Our house-sitters are starting to leave us happy notes about cute things Clementine does when we are away from home—a great improvement over their earlier notes about her behavior that could be read only as veiled threats of mutiny.

As we write this, she is about to turn two years old. Two years is so little time, yet we feel like she has been part of our lives forever. A week ago we celebrated our twenty-seventh wedding anniversary. Jane baked the chocolate cake we always have and we bought some nice gifts for each other. But the best gift came from Clementine, who ran into Michael's office early on our anniversary morning as he was sitting down to write. She began pacing back and forth. "Sit down,"

Michael said, but she continued to pace. "Go to your place!" Michael ordered, walking her out the office door into the hallway. In a few seconds she was back, pacing again. Michael looked at her intently, trying to figure out this relapse of behavior. He noticed she looked uncomfortable. He got up from his chair and walked her to the stairs. She bounded down ahead of him and ran full speed until she got to the back door. As soon as it was opened, she scurried out and made a bowel movement on the lawn. Michael let her in, praised her, and gave her a pat on the head. At that, she walked to her bed, made the requisite nesting shuffle, and sank into it with a sigh of relief.

As her puppy years are fading, Clementine has at long last developed a superego. With this one act we knew that she had finally learned right from wrong, and she knew to come to us for help. She will never be Lassie, never clever enough to tell Mother that Timmy has fallen into the well, but she is smart enough to live responsibly in our home, and that's enough.

A turd in the yard would not normally make our list of great anniversary gifts, but in this case we could not think of anything more blessedly symbolic of family togetherness. Just as she was about to leave the grace state of puppyhood, Clementine finally had become a welcome part of the family pack. She had learned our language and we had learned hers. Peace, it's wonderful.

Ode to a Lost Puppy

When I saw him—young, ardent, and believing—bringing me, in some wise, from the depths of unwearied nature, quite fresh news of life and trusting and wonderstruck, as though he had been the first of his race that came to inaugurate the earth and as though we were still in the first days of the world's existence, I envied the gladness of his certainty.

—Maurice Maeterlinck, *Our Friend the Dog* (1904)

Appendices

POPULAR PUPPIES

Breeds get popular for reasons other than their good looks, useful skills, or suitability as household pets.

Sometimes the charisma of a well-liked owner rubs off, as happened to Franklin D. Roosevelt's White House pet, Fala, who helped make Scotties one of the top-ten most popular breeds in the 1930s. A Bulldog breeder we know recalls that shortly after Captain and Tennille's first album was released—featuring a cover photo of the singers with their Bulldog—phone calls started coming in from people who wanted a "Captain and Tennille dog."

Sometimes a dog's media-manufactured personality generates a groundswell of interest. By the time the cult-fave TV show *Baa Baa Blacksheep* returned to the air in 1977 as the *Black Sheep Squadron,* prominently featuring a Bull Terrier as part of its group of devil-may-care flyboys, puppy wait lists were already growing at Bull Terrier breeders around the country. Similarly, the scrappy "white cavalier" got a big boost from the prominence of macho-cute beer salesdog Spuds MacKenzie. Fans of Spuds's suds wanted a dog with his anthropomorphic savoir-faire and apparently assumed that all Bull Terriers had it.

It also happens that breeds get popular because popular culture creates an irresistible urge to own them. The best known example is Lassie, a character created in 1938 in Eric Knight's short story, "Lassie Come Home," which was expanded into an international best-selling children's book, then made into seven movies, a radio drama, and a TV series. Thanks to this incredibly successful fictional Collie (always, curiously, played by male dogs, not bitches), the image of the breed went from that of a working sheep dog to a family's most faithful friend.

More recently, when *101 Dalmatians* was rereleased in the fall of 1996, thousands of those who saw it were so smitten that they went out and bought a Dalmatian puppy for Christmas.

Yes, indeed: Dalmatians can be adorable, as the movie showed. What the movie did not show is that they also can be epileptic, suffer dermatitis, and grow kidney stones; nearly one out of ten is deaf; and many are high-strung and don't like children. Not *all* Dalmatians exhibit such problems. A well-bred "coach hound" (a moniker derived from their former occupation as traveling companions) can be a magnificent pet. The 1949 *Modern Dog Encyclopedia* described the breed as a perfect dog for the suburbs—"strikingly handsome, faithful to the family, neither obtrusive nor shy around strangers, generally possessed of remarkable intelligence, and clean of habit inside the house and outdoors."

The problem is that when a breed suddenly gets popular, the demand for it inevitably results in a supply of puppies begotten for no reason other than to cash in. With a mere sixty-three-day gestation period, dogs of any breed are fairly easy to produce fast . . . if the breeder is willing to mate just about any able-bodied male and female and to breed and sell all their puppies with no regard for genetic consequences. Intensive line-breeding (mating grandfathers to granddaughters, granddams to grandsons) or the use of studs and brood bitches of inferior constitution not only perpetuates but actually amplifies hereditary weakness.

Pop culture notoriety can be the worst thing for a breed, polluting the gene pool for generations. Devotees of the German Shepherd rue the fame of Rin-Tin-Tin (played by several dogs) in movies and on television, indirectly blaming his renown for the gradual erosion of the fine working-dog temperament that originally had been cultivated by German farmers who needed a strong canine helpmate. After World War II, the shepherd's showring success and subsequent popularity in this country further compromised his physical prowess, for judges traditionally gave the blue ribbon to dogs with dramatically down-sloping hindquarters. Breeding for this "sleek" look, a grotesque exaggeration of proper German Shepherd posture, helped firmly instill in the breed's American bloodlines a tendency toward crippling hip dysplasia. Today in this country, many aficionados who breed German Shepherds will boast of studs and brood bitches from overseas, where the breed was not corrupted by careless reproduction.

In hopes of avoiding such a fate, the Jack Russell Club of America came out firmly *against* AKC recognition of their breed, believing that such an endorsement (which became official on January 1, 1998) is sure to encourage people to willy-nilly buy and breed a kind of dog that is definitely not for everyone. Originally designed as a fearless and fairly ferocious hunting dog, the little Jack Russell went for decades in relative obscurity, unrecognized by the AKC, its feisty personality and general good health kept secure by a small cadre of responsible breeders. For those who have cared for the Jack Russell Terrier—maintaining its unique personality and physique—to mainstream it is a recipe for disaster. So they gnash their teeth over the celebrity status of Max, the JRT who costarred with Jim Carrey in *The Mask* and the spectacularly well-trained JRT named Eddie featured in the hit TV show *Frasier.* "He's Hot. He's Sexy. He's Purebred," exclaimed Eddie's cover story in *Entertainment Weekly.* Predictably, *Frasier's* star dog has caused the population of JRTs in America to grow dramatically.

Of all the breeds to enjoy sudden media-generated popularity, few are less likely candidates for ordinary pethood than the JRT. Even people fortunate enough to buy a physically sound example might find themselves unpleasantly surprised when they discover that it is NOT characteristic for a healthy JRT to sit contentedly in the living room for long periods watching TV as does *Frasier's* Eddie. More typical behavior for the breed is to bark all day, dig holes in the ground, chase anything that moves, and bite a child that dares to pull its tail or ears. "Please remember," the Jack Russell Terrier Club of America implores potential buyers, "Russell Rescue is very busy with displaced terriers because MANY PEOPLE UNDERESTIMATE LIFE WITH A JACK RUSSELL TERRIER!"

As for all the Dalmatians people bought in the wake of the Walt Disney movie, *The New York Times* estimated that within a year of the movie's rerelease, the number of abandoned Dalmatians in shelters nationwide had doubled. In the fall of 1997, the Dalmatian Rescue Resources Site on the Internet posted this sign above the picture of a forlorn spotted dog in a Humane Society cage: "Dalmatians are dying in shelters all over the USA."

Conclusion: Buy a purebred puppy only after you have considered the pros *and cons* of that breed, never because it is popular. And if you happen to like a breed that does become popular, be all the more vigilant about getting one from a devoted and responsible breeder.

THE BREED FINDER:

A Chart to Help Choose the Right Breed of Dog

Use this chart only as a starting point. Remember that, like we humans, every dog is an individual and every bloodline has its own peculiar traits.

You are . . .	Consider this breed	. . . for these reasons.	But Consider these Caveats
A couch potato with a small apartment	Chihuahua	pocket-sized; a good sentry	barks; dislikes other dogs
A runner who wants company	Borzoi	loves to run	tireless; needs to run at liberty
A suburban family with young children	Golden Retriever	sensible, gentle, easily trained	will happily track mud into house
Weak or infirm	Pug	small, tractable, easy keeper	stand-offish
Allergic to dogs	Chinese Crested Dog	nearly hairless single-layer coat	bare skin requires care; can sunburn
A man who wants to pick up women	West Highland Terrier	cute, cuddly, but not effeminate	a busy character; needs attention
A woman who wants to pick up men	Bull Terrier	a macho, drinking-buddy dog	dog-to-dog aggression
Hostile and alone and like it like that	Tibetan Mastiff	vicious and destructive	looks cute; might attract people
Fastidious about your clothes or furniture	Dalmatian	short-haired, tidy	hyperactive; many are deaf
Clumsy and dangerous to all living things	Boxer	agile enough to avoid injury	can drool and snore

You Want . . .	Consider this breed	. . . for these reasons.	But consider these caveats
A dog to protect you on city streets	Rottweiler	scares bad guys to death	needs training and firm guidance
A dog to guard your country home	Great Dane	formidable and athletic	eats like a horse; doesn't live long
A dog that will entertain you	Poodle	bright, eager to amuse	needs grooming and a social life
The most dog in the least amount of space	Pomeranian	a six-pound dynamo	demands lots of attention
A dog that requires minimum attention	Chow Chow	confident, independent	can have a will of its own
A codependent love-slave	Greyhound	lives to be loved and pampered	needs space and exercise
A dog that will make you its love-slave	Shih Tzu	bred to be worshipped	needs regular grooming
A companion for a preexisting pet	Labrador Retriever	sensible and nonpossessive	can be headstrong
A fashion statement	Afghan Hound	silky long coat, hypnotic gait	chases anything that moves
A sympathetic, psychiatric presence	Bullmastiff	looks sad and worried	drools, snores, farts

You Need . . .	Consider this breed	. . . for these reasons.	But consider these caveats
A dog that doesn't bark	Basenji	ululates instead of barks	fights with other dogs
A dog that can live outdoors year-around	Siberian Husky	adapts to any climate	not emotionally outgoing
A dog with no medical problems	a mutt	strength of genetic diversity	no snob appeal; unknown genes
A conversation piece	Puli	corded Rasta hair; waterproof	drags pounds of mud into house
A dog to find lost people and things	Bloodhound	great sense of smell	drools like crazy

Dorothy Harrison Eustis
and Morris Frank

America's Guide Dog Movement Begins

In the fall of 1927, a blind young Tennessean named Morris Frank was navigating the streets of Nashville, led along by an attendant and using his cane to feel for a curb. "Hey, Mr. Frank, there's a piece in this week's *Post* you oughta read!" called out Charlie the corner newsboy. "It's about blind folks like you."

Frank gave Charlie a nickel for the magazine. He later wrote: "That five cents bought an article that was worth more than a million dollars to me."

At home in the evening, as Frank's mother sat by his side, his father read him the story, titled "The Seeing Eye." Its author, Dorothy Harrison Eustis, was an American breeder of German Shepherds who marveled at Germany's ground-breaking work training dogs to lead its blinded war veterans. At the time, there was nothing at all like this program in the U.S., where even the most independent blind people were forced to rely on white canes and the kindness of human attendants. Frank recalled his and his parents' reaction: "We sat silent for a moment. Then all began talking at once. Our words overlapped, knocked into one another as flint against flint, ignited and lighted a once gloomy room with the blessed brightness of hope. After that evening, life was never the same for any of us."

When he was read the story, Morris Frank was twenty years old, blinded from a blow during a boxing match when he was sixteen. Although he was already gainfully employed, he was immensely frustrated by the limits imposed on him by his blindness. He hated always needing to depend on attendants who were at best impatient, at worst, pitying.

"If what we read about these wonder-working dogs was really true, they could free a person," Frank wrote. "A companionable dog . . . could ease the bitterness I felt at losing my sight. . . . I visualized myself walking freely down the street. I would be able to make calls on prospective clients for my insurance business without the encumbrance of a talkative, incompatible guide. I could go to college on my own. I could even have a date—and it would not have to be a double date. . . . There must be young men like me all over America who longed to break out of the prison of blindness. These dogs would liberate us all."

The morning after his father read him "The Seeing Eye," Morris Frank wrote to Dorothy Eustis, who was living in Switzerland, and pleaded to her, "Train me and I will bring back my dog and show people here how a blind man can be absolutely on his own." Eager to tell the world what she had found, Mrs. Eustis invited him to visit her in Switzerland. After an intensive period of training with a guide dog named Buddy, Frank finally declared, "I'm free, by God, I'm free!" He and Buddy returned to the United States, where they traveled the country to show people the miracle he had discovered. His account of learning to work with a trained guide dog was told in his 1957 book, *First Lady of the Seeing Eye;* and through his efforts, the first program to train dogs for the blind was established in 1929 as The Seeing Eye in Morristown, New Jersey.

The very public success of Morris Frank and of the training school he inspired has made "Seeing Eye Dog" a virtually generic term for all dogs trained to lead blind people. Today there are well over a dozen schools that train guide dogs in North America (see p.183), all using the basic principles related by Mrs. Eustis in her article. But only those from the school in Morristown are correctly called Seeing Eye Dogs.

Guiding Eyes Facts
and Stats

- Guiding Eyes for the Blind, headquartered in Yorktown Heights, New York, was founded in 1954. More than 4,500 guide dog teams have graduated since then.
- Applicants for a Guiding Eyes dog must be at least sixteen years old. There is no maximum age limit.
- 160 student–guide dog teams graduate each year. Tuition for all students is free. All costs are paid for by donations to the school.
- The cost of breeding, raising, and training one guide dog is $25,000.
- More than 500 volunteer puppy-raising families along the East Coast nurture Guiding Eyes puppies.
- The on-campus Guiding Eyes kennel houses a complete veterinary facility and accommodations for 150 dogs.
- Graduation ceremonies, held once each month on a Saturday at 1:30pm on the Yorktown Heights Campus, are open to the public.

Guiding Eyes for the Blind
611 Granite Springs Road
Yorktown Heights, NY 10598
(914)245-4024
(800)942-0149
fax: (914)245-1609

The Guiding Eyes Breeding Center: (914)878-3330—Call them if you are interested in raising a puppy.

Office of Alumni Relations: (914)243-2215—Call if you want to volunteer at the school.

Office of Development: (914)243-2227—Call if you want to donate to the school or make a bequest.

GUIDE DOG SCHOOLS

Canine Vision Canada
Box 907
Oakville, Ontario, Canada L6J5E8
(416)842-2891

Eye Dog Foundation
512 N. Larchmont Boulevard
Los Angeles, CA 90004
(213)468-1012

Eye of the Pacific Guide Dogs
747 Amana Street
Honolulu, HI 96814
(808)941-1088

Fidelco Guide Dog Foundation
Box 142
Bloomfield, CT 06002
(203)243-5200

Guide Dogs for the Blind
Box 151200
San Rafael, CA 94915
(415)499-4000

Guide Dog Foundation for the Blind
371 E. Jericho Turnpike
Smithtown, NY 11787
(516)265-2121

Guide Dogs of the Desert
Box 1692
Palm Springs, CA 92263
(619)329-6257

Guiding Eyes for the Blind
611 Granite Springs Road
Yorktown Heights, NY 10598
(914)245-4024

International Guiding Eyes
13445 GlenOaks Boulevard
Sylmar, CA 91342
(818)362-5834

Kansas Specialty Dog Service
123 W. 7th, Box 216
Washington, KS 66969
(913)325-2256

Leader Dogs for the Blind
1039 S. Rochester Road
Rochester, MI 48307
(313)651-9011

Pilot Dogs
625 West Town Street
Columbus, OH 43215
(614)221-6367

The Seeing Eye
Washington Valley Road
Morristown, NJ 07960
(201)539-4425

Southeastern Guide Dogs
4210 77th Street East
Palmetto, FL 34221
(941)729-6646

Canine Companions
for Independence

Leading blind people is just one way dogs serve humans with special needs. Canine Companions for Independence is a California-based organization with four training centers around the country that breed puppies who are raised and taught to assist people with disabilities other than blindness. Their canine graduates, who are mostly labs and Golden Retrievers but have also included Pembroke Welsh Corgis and shelties, fall into these categories:

- Service Dogs. Trained to perform practical tasks, such as opening cabinets or flipping light switches for people with limited use of their arms or fetching things for individuals in wheelchairs, service dogs are placed permanently with individuals in much the same way Guiding Eyes dogs are placed with the blind.
- Hearing Dogs. Hearing dogs, sometimes called "signal dogs," are trained to alert otherwise able people who are deaf or hearing-impaired to such audio events as ringing telephones, smoke alarms, a crying baby, a doorbell, or an alarm clock.
- Facility Dogs. These are dogs trained to work with professionals who use them to help people with developmental disabilities. Such dogs have proven especially useful for work with withdrawn souls who sometimes can respond to the presence of a friendly, nonjudgmental canine in ways they cannot respond to humans.

For more information, contact:

Canine Companions for Independence
Box 446
Santa Rosa, CA 95402
(800)572-BARK

Puppy Bibliography

Hundreds of experts have written books that explain how to have a successful relationship with a puppy. This is a short list of some titles we believe worth looking into. Some are puppy-specific, but we also have included some favorites about dog-people relationships in general.

If you are considering acquisition of a purebred and want to compare and contrast the official standards of each AKC-recognized breed, read *The Roger Caras Dog Book: A Complete Guide to Every AKC Breed* by Roger Caras (M. Evans). Also of interest is *The Complete Dog Book* by the American Kennel Club. It is the purebred bible, and like the Holy Bible, its focus is more on the glories of its subject than on mundane imperfections; for the latter, talk to people who have lived with the breed you are considering.

PUPPY-SPECIFIC BOOKS

The Art of Raising a Puppy by the Monks of New Skete (Little, Brown)
The Chosen Puppy: How to Select and Raise a Great Puppy from an Animal Shelter by Carol Lea Benjamin (Howell)
Civilizing Your Puppy by Barbara J. Wrede (Barrons)
Complete Guide to Puppy Care by Mark Evans (MacMillan)
Every Puppy: Perfect Pet or Perfect Pest? by Eric Allan (Howell)
How to Raise a Puppy You Can Live With by Clarice Rutherford and David H. Neil (Alpine Press)
How to Train Your Puppy by Barbara Woodhouse (Seven Hills)
I Just Got a Puppy: What Do I Do? by Mordecai Siegal and Matthew Margolis (Fireside)
Perfect Puppy: How to Choose Your Dog by Its Behavior by Ben Hart, Lynette Hart, and Benjamin L. Hart (W. H. Freeman)
The Perfect Puppy by Gwen Bailey (Readers Digest)
Pet Owner's Guide to Puppy Care and Training by John Holmes and Mary Holmes (Howell)

Puppy Care and Training: An Owner's Guide to a Happy Healthy Pet by Bardi McLennan (Howell)

Puppy Preschool: Raising Your Puppy Right, Right from the Start! by John Ross and Barbara McKinney (St. Martin's)

The Puppy Report: How to Select a Healthy, Happy Dog by Larry Shook (Ballantine)

Superdog: Raising the Perfect Canine Companion by Michael Fox (Howell)

Surviving Your Dog's Adolescence by Carol Lea Benjamin (Howell)

What to Name Your Dog by Carrie Shook (Howell)

You and Your Puppy: Training and Health Care for Puppy's First Year by James Debitetto and Sarah Hodgson (Howell)

GENERAL DOG BOOKS

201 Ways to Enjoy Your Dog: A Complete Guide to Organized US and Canadian Activities for Dog Lovers by Ellie Milon (Alpine Press)

A-To-Z of Dogs and Puppies by Barbara Woodhouse (Stein & Day)

Doglopaedia: A Complete Guide to Dog Care by Job Michael Evans and Kay White (MacMillan)

Dogs for Dummies by Gina Spadafori (IDG)

How to be Your Dog's Best Friend by the Monks of New Skete (Little, Brown)

Man Meets Dog by Konrad Lorenz (Kodansha)

Mother Knows Best: The Natural Way to Train Your Dog by Carol Lea Benjamin (Howell/Macmillan)

People, Pooches, and Problems by Job Michael Evans (Howell)

Second-Hand Dog: How to Turn Yours into a First-Rate Pet by Carol Lea Benjamin (Howell)

The Tellington Ttouch: A Revolutionary Natural Method to Train and Care for Your Favorite Animal by Linda Tellington-Jones and Sybil Taylor (Penguin)

Training and Explaining: How to Be the Dog Trainer You Want to Be by Job Michael Evans (Howell)

Understanding and Training Your Dog or Puppy by H. Ellen Whiteley (Crown)

If you have access to the Internet, one of the best resources for finding out about dog shows, sporting trials, and details of breed registration, as well as for learning general health and pet-care tips or perusing the official standard of all AKC-registered breeds is the American Kennel Club's web site:

http://www.akc.org/. Here you will also find contact information for national and local breed clubs, through which you can find responsible breeders if you are in the market for a puppy.

Two other great cyberspace resources are the Usenet group Rec.pets.dogs, and its abundant FAQ page, the address of which is http://WWW. Zmall.Com/pet/dog-faqs/. The latter has countless links to breed-specific sites as well as sites devoted to dog sports, canine health care, traveling with dogs, and even dog-related humor.